"Heartstopping—a piercing, bittersweet picture of what it was really like in the hot center of the literary, jazz and art world that was downtown Bohemian New York as the fifties became the sixties."

—Sara Blackburn

"A feminist scrutiny such as this is just what those last decades needed, as the beats themselves needed it."

—Lawrence Ferlinghetti

"This is a great read, moving, joyous, painful. It's the story of a daughter, lover and mother set in the Village. Hettie lives on the edge, in the heart of the new jazz, poetry, politics and life. At last a book about the fifties and sixties from a feminist that covers sex, race, and class and the ups and downs of daily existence."

—Rosalyn Baxandall, author of *Words on Fire*

"Hettie Jones has written a rare and valuable book, a personal story that works equally as history. Her memoir is the memoir of an important artistic and political milieu; it's possibly the best account yet written of what it was like to be at the center of New York Bohemianism in the 1950s and 1960s. Her honesty and forgiveness and the clarity of her writing are exemplary and moving."

—Russell Banks

"Rooted in a time when issues of race and religion (but not yet gender) were forcing their way into public consciousness, Jones' story draws its strength from a woman's search for her poetic voice amid the tidal waves of change."

—Cindy Hirschfeld, *Trenton Times*

"She certainly has told it like it was! . . . The book serves to remind us of how many strong currents there were that sweep into our lives today; how much vitality there was in our lives in our chaotic youth; and how many issues were set in relief and struggled with and are still with us."

—Dore Ashton, author of *The New York School: A Cultural Reckoning*

HOW I BECAME HETTIE JONES

HETTIE JONES

HOW I BECAME

HETTIE JONES

Grove Press ▼ New York

Originally published in 1990 by E. P. Dutton, a division of
Penguin Books USA Inc.
First Grove Press edition published in 1997

Published simultaneously in Canada
Printed in the United States of America

Library of Congress Cataloging-in-Publication Data
Jones, Hettie
How I became Hettie Jones / Hettie Jones.
p.   cm.
ISBN 0-8021-3496-3
1. Jones, Hettie—Biography.   2. Baraka, Imamu Amiri, 1934–
—Marriage.   3. Women authors, American—20th century—
Biography.   4. Authors' spouses—United States—Biography.
I. Title.
PS3560.0485Z47   1997
818'.5409—dc20
[B]   96-32006

Design by Margo D. Barooshian

Grove Press
841 Broadway
New York, NY 10003

10 9 8 7 6 5 4 3 2 1

for my daughters, Kellie and Lisa

pat my bro
pat my sister
see we tender
women
live
on

I owe this book to Berenice Hoffman, first, for her faith, to Joyce Johnson for her example, Helene Dorn for saving my letters, Dorothy White for standing by, and to Joyce Engelson, my editor, who waited fifteen years for me to write it.

Conversations with Steve Cannon, Fielding Dawson, and Basil and Martha King were helpful; the assistance of Margaret Wolf invaluable; the support of Cora Coleman, Coyt L. Jones, and the late Anna Lois Jones immeasurable. Thanks to everyone who calls me Mom, and to all the many missing names: if you were there then please come in.

HOW I BECAME
HETTIE JONES

Meet Hettie Cohen. I'm sitting at an ancient rolltop desk that's stuffed to its top compartments with manuscripts and envelopes and all the related litter of magazine production, and I have no idea that this will be with me for years after I've become Hettie Jones.

Nearby, running half the length of a cluttered storefront office, is a six-foot-high row of wooden milk crates, housing old 78 rpm jazz records in crumbling paper sleeves. Flakes of this yellow-brown stuff drift down and settle like snow on the dirty linoleum, and the smell of it masks the casual funk from a darker back room, where Richard (Dick) Hadlock, editor of the *Record Changer*, the magazine published here, sleeps whenever he's not with his girlfriend.

But he's with her now—or somewhere—leaving me: Hettie Cohen, a small, dark, twenty-two-year-old Jew from Laurelton, Queens, with a paperback book in my hand. Kafka's *Amerika*. I'm the Subscription Manager and I'm about to interview an applicant for the job of Shipping Manager. It's March 1957 in Greenwich Village. A haphazard pile of boxes, holding unsold issues, partly obscures the unwashed front (and only) window of the store. From time to time I glance toward this pale daylight, up from *Amerika*, waiting.

The applicant, arrived on a gust of sweet afternoon, turned out to be a young black man, no surprise. It was he who was surprised. "You're reading Kafka!" he said happily. He was small and wiry, with a widow's peak that sharpened his close-cut hair, and a mustache and goatee to match. Yet the rakishness of all these triangles was set back, made reticent, by a button-down shirt and Clark's shoes. A Brooks Brothers look. I sat him down and we started to talk. He was smart, and very direct, and for emphasis stabbed the air with his third—not index—finger, an affectation to notice, of course. But his movements were easy, those of a man at home not only in skin but in muscle and bone. And he led with his head. What had started with Kafka just went on going.

An hour later, when Dick arrived, we were still talking. "Did you tell him about the job?" Dick asked me.

"The job?" I echoed, and blushed. Left responsible and gone derelict. No interview. I see myself, now, as the heat invades my face, a hand up to my open, astonished mouth. To the left is my subscription corner, the typewriter, unanswered mail. And on my right LeRoi Jones—square-jawed, pointy-browed, grinning at me shyly, and still, I think, a little surprised I'd had so much to say.

"The idea . . . is to change first of our own volition and according to our own inner promptings before they impose completely arbitrary changes on us."
—JANE BOWLES,
Two Serious Ladies, 1943

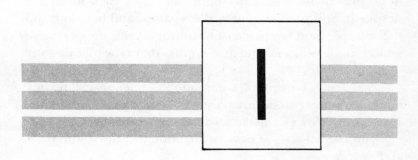

I started leaving home when I was six and weighed thirty-eight pounds. Lying on a mountainside, where my sister and I were at summer camp, I had my hands in the air pretending to weave the clouds, as I had that morning begun weaving a basket.

The basket was on my mind. The night before at the lake I'd been shown the reed, soaking, beautiful as it was, presumptuous to alter. But in the morning the damp, pliant skein and the texture had thrilled me. For two years I'd played piano and tap-danced, but the basket seemed the very shape of my pleasure in doing, or making. Which pleasure was more important to me than any other feeling.

It surpassed my love for my family, and at home I was guilty about it.

At camp this guilt had gone and there was such relief from home, where my parents' bickering knotted the air. My mother was smart and right; my father would have fun in his life. I already knew that loving them equally didn't help, that theirs wasn't my fight, that they each loved me despite it. Still I hated their endless natter, and here at camp the soft, pleasant language of encouragement, the pervasive good humor, was as sweet as the grass that now pillowed my head.

Suddenly I heard a commotion, someone calling my name, and there stood my parents! Come to take me home, I was sure. Why else make a whole day's journey?

But the basket—to have to abandon it! I burst into tears and ran.

Later, after the explanation that they had simply come to visit, my mother embraced me. "I knew that was you from the top of the hill," she said. "You were the one with her hands up, making shapes in the air." But I knew she didn't understand that this love of mine would have to take me away from her.

In Laurelton, the finished basket stayed among cans of string beans and boxes of cornflakes and the salami hung to dry on its string, in a pantry with a narrow window onto a porch. I never carried a key to the house, and if, as sometimes happened, my mother went out and forgot to leave the key in the milk box, I would boost myself up and wriggle through this window, trying not to knock over the pickle jars or catch my foot in the high, braided handle of the basket, which was never put to much use. Banished, it lost magic.

When my mother was out she was often volunteering— for the Red Cross, or the Girl Scouts, or various Zionist causes; eventually she chaired her local Hadassah, then all of Long Island. Amazing to me now, I never once saw her in action. What we did together was shop. My mother, born Lottie Lewis, was a small woman with aspirations to quality, who sewed like a master tailor but was barely a journeyman cook—I saw my first clove of garlic only after I'd left her house. She liked the pictures in *House Beautiful*, the stories in *Reader's Digest*, and her treat was the Broadway play: she'd put on her mink and her amethysts, and take the train to meet my father in the city. But she never had a maid, and for many years she washed the family's clothes by hand in a sink in the cellar. Sometimes she hummed a little, ironing in the kitchen on the board that pulled out from the wall. Companionably, I ironed beside her when I came home from school: first I learned pillowcases, then handkerchiefs, then slips with lacy edges. I loved my mother, except when she attacked my father, and she was always good for a hug. But if in my passionate way I went on too long, she'd sigh and call me "musher," and unwrap my arms.

And she wasn't much help. I was ten when I tried to show her a magazine article I'd read about menses. "Look," I suggested. My mother, at the foot of the stairs, glanced at the magazine and went on up. "Well, now you know," she said over her shoulder. About sex she told me nothing; of men she said only: "Marry someone who loves you more." She, for one, should have known how that fails. But I never thought about marriage. I had other plans and love was all I wanted.

I felt kin to my father's soul, his broader humor and bodily ease. He was a short, barrelly, dark-skinned man named Oscar, who boasted a jaunty grace—he did Charlie Chaplin's wobbly walk and any dance from the two-step to the rhumba. He and one of his brothers had a loft full of pounding presses near Union Square in Manhattan, where they man-ufactured advertising displays—tall cardboard cutouts on easels, stands for sunglasses. Sometimes, after shopping at Ohrbach's and Klein's with my mother, I'd be taken around

7

the corner to that thunder and inky perfume. There was even a special, temperamental machine that all by itself made a case for your pocket comb. It could only be fixed by my second-youngest uncle, temperamental himself—a nighttime cabbie, sometime carny—with whom, like that machine, I was terribly, singly, in love.

Weekdays my father left on the early train and came home at night with the paper under his arm; Saturdays he brought a roll of bills in his pocket. Predictably in through the side door, petting the dog and forgetting to wipe his feet. Though he had my sympathy, he was impatient with all and sundry, cursing the storm windows he had to put up, driving like a cowboy. Only in sports could he fling his arms to effect, and he taught us—my sister and I both lefties like him—to throw and catch and fly-fish. In his arms I learned to love water. He took me to Ebbets Field and Yankee Stadium. One day, left to mind me, he took me to the races at Belmont, though he knew I was underage. Refused admission, he gave me to the woman in whose driveway he'd parked the car, who promised to sneak me in. I'd never been left with a Christian before. But then this cheerful, adventurous woman tramped me through sweet-smelling fields, and squeezed me past a board fence—and there I soon was, beside my grinning Daddy, the only kid at the Belmont Raceway!

But Oscar and I, joined at the heart, were separated at the head. There were only a couple of books in our house; he'd never read them or any others and wouldn't. Once, catching me at it, he pointed to the pages in my hand and said, "You won't find life there."

But there wasn't much for me in Laurelton, where we'd come from polyglot Brooklyn; no Negroes, Hispanics, Italians, only some Anglos and Irish who couldn't afford to move away from the Jews. I went to school with their children, but never to their homes. There was a firm inevitability to

8

this; you just didn't mix, exactly the way you didn't serve milk with meat.

The milk/meat rule was all that remained of the kosher laws. My parents spoke Yiddish only to hide things. Even in English they rarely referred to a past. Their families had come from Poland, or was it Russia, they weren't sure. And Brooklyn was nothing to speak of either, as if poverty rendered you undeserving of history. At night, in my narrow maple bed, under the starched, white, ruffled, pink-ribbon-threaded spread my mother had made, I'd make up stories with myself as the hero of great, seafaring adventures. The only hint I ever had of my future was on our every other Sunday trip to Newark, to visit my mother's family, when we'd stop for a sandwich at Katz's on the Lower East Side. "Send a salami to your boy in the Army" read the signs, but I cared less for the food than for the long, mysterious reach of Houston Street, the way it seemed to hold, river to river, some secret old New York that hadn't ceased to exist, not the way you were led to think. Laurelton never spoke of that place, just as they never would see my return to it. But I could see, from our round gray 1946 Chrysler, some streets I would have liked to set foot on. I could even have caught a quick piece of the Village before we cut a sharp left and left it all behind at the Holland Tunnel.

My sister, Susan, olive-skinned with flaxen hair and royal blue eyes, was told and told again how her looks would bring her a wealthy husband to change her life. But she clung to her childhood sweetheart, and married him at twenty.

I was fourteen then and leaving on my own, as soon as possible. I passed the test for Music and Art High School, though the piano piece I played was called "Malagueña," and the teacher, with a sniff, said, "Where is your Bach?" But Music and Art, in Manhattan, would have meant a two-hour trip. Far Rockaway High, where I got beached instead, was a fifty-minute ride on the Long Island Railroad. I bided

9

my time in the smoking car, underexposed and smoldering. I no longer knew what music I wanted to play. When I improvised something atonal I thought of as "modern," my mother would call, gaily: "That doesn't sound like practicing!" I began to hang out in the lunchroom with boys who talked anarchy.

By 1951, the year we were labeled the Silent Generation, I'd been recommended to silence often. Men had little use for an outspoken woman, I'd been warned. What I wanted, I was told, was security and upward mobility, which might be mine if I learned to shut my mouth. Myself I simply expected, by force of will, to assume a new shape in the future. Unlike any woman in my family or anyone I'd ever actually known, I was going to *become*—something, anything, whatever that meant.

To accomplish this I felt the need to cloister myself for a while, away from the usual expectations, at what was known as an "all-girls college." Accepted at Vassar I chose instead Mary Washington, the woman's college of the University of Virginia. I made this decision from pictures only. I had some vague suspicion that Vassar might make me a snob, and the South was cheaper and farther from home.

My parents waved good-bye at Penn Station. I had never been farther south than Freehold, New Jersey, where my second-oldest uncle had a chicken farm. It was September 1951. I had just turned seventeen.

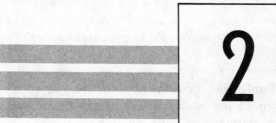

A haze of late summer heat lay over sleepy little Fredericksburg, Virginia. I tumbled into a taxi, sweating all over my new Royal portable, assailed by the heavy, sweet, southern air. The young woman with whom I was sharing the ride smiled. She said:

"MahnaimesLuvlis, whusyoahs?"

The pictures hadn't lied; the campus was beautiful, the architecture faithful to Thomas Jefferson's original design for the university—where the men were—sixty miles away in Charlottesville. The Mary Washington students, all white, were from various southern and western states.

And there was I—alone with the *goyim*!

I was shocked right out of my self-absorption. Before I

could think of myself I had to look *out*. Jesus seemed to be everywhere. I had to learn to put down my knife when I ate, to pour and hand tea. These were the people of white gloves and horse breeds, who had patterns of culture officially, including formal dinners and vespers; Mary Washington was George's mother. But the military furnished her imagery—the book of rules was called *The Bayonet*. I felt very much the Yankee Jew from New York. In the dining room, with a kind of tense awe, I was asked, "Are you Puerto Rican?" The roommates to whom I'd been assigned weren't pleased.

But friendly faces surfaced, the best a Tennessee hillbilly, Linda, a rangy blonde with prominent teeth who loved to drive fast; she showed me back roads, country music and the blues. She tried patiently to teach me to hold my liquor. On a visit to her home, after a train ride through the strange, slag-heaped shame of Appalachia, I had my first, rich, pork-flavored taste of greens. The South seemed a world to itself of pain and pleasure.

And in its confines I seemed unique. In my dorm a black woman who worked as a maid sometimes picked up extra money ironing. As I had with my mother, I ironed beside her. She seemed to understand, smiled when she saw me coming, and showed me how to handle the tucks in my blouses. Apart from her, I met no other black people regularly.

As a drama major I learned carpentry and electricity, how to pull a curtain and how to climb a ladder in a skirt (pants weren't permitted; after protest, we were issued mechanic's overalls). My height prohibited serious roles—I played a comic Russian officer in *Arms and the Man*, and in *Our Town* a small, dead boy. But live I performed for children in backwoods schoolrooms, sang and played the piano for sad old men in veterans' hospitals, wrote class shows, had a radio program. One night, awed by the reach of my own arm, I led a thousand young women in song.

But this was just power, I felt, not the heart of the matter, and though I longed to write the plays of Lorca, I began with poems. We lived two or three to a room with one desk, so I spent my nights in the basement office of the yearbook (*The Battlefield*), drinking tap water instant coffee under a poster that said, Tomorrow's Leaders Need Help Today. With a razor and to great effect, I thought, I cut my hair in an odd, pointed fringe, and on my feet wore Girl Scout oxfords that seemed, to me, the perfect signal of a new, sexy but surefooted woman. And when interviewed by the school newspaper (*The Bullet*), I declared myself a "mutation," since there didn't seem to be anyone like me, either where I'd come from or where I was presently. In my senior year my poems were published in the literary magazine (*The Epaulet*), and I wrote a thesis on "The Poet in the Theater."

Graduated, both of us en route to New York and graduate school at Columbia, Linda and I detoured to Richmond, Virginia, where we worked for a man named Harold, who put out crews to sell electric fans. Black and white, we were driven to rural roads and set down. I traveled long, unsuccessful miles. Harold said something was wrong with me, that I was the only Jew in America to come down South and never make a nickel. Which did not keep him out of my bed: evenings he'd give Linda his car while he taught me wonderful things. Though he never did teach me to sell, so I had thirteen cents in my pocket this one morning. I was lounging with my back to the car door, Linda was opposite me in the driver's seat. There were two black women in the back we'd just met, and now she and they are talking about their skin. "Heh heh heh," laughs hillbilly Linda, "Millie, have you really got a tan?" To which Millie, laughing herself, replies, "My friends don't even recognize my face!" And then the three of them fall out in giggles, as if the concept of blackness itself were vastly comedic. And there, now, as she turns to include me, is the sparkle in Linda's eyes. It's a strange, excited shine, a dirty secret. I don't know it. What is it?

Skin.

Later that afternoon, tired, I found myself alone on a dirt road. The heat was oppressive, the fan I was carrying cut into my hand. I'd passed some houses ten minutes back but there didn't seem to be any more coming up. Out of some tall grass at the roadside a little black girl appeared, seven or eight years old, barefoot, dressed in a cotton smock. She waited as I approached and then asked, pointing to the fan, "What are you doing with that?"

"I'm selling them," I said.

"Oh, come to *my* house," she said dramatically, and with that thrust her hand into mine. I looked down. I'd never held a black person's hand. It was dry, dusty, sweet, and so fragile, and dark as I was from that southern sun it wasn't that different from mine. Skin, I thought, remembering Linda.

It's strange, now, to consider what that hand may have meant. As an outsider Jew I could have tried for white, aspired to the liberal intellectual, potentially conservative Western tradition. But I never was drawn to that history, and with so little specific to call my own I felt free to choose. Maybe all the small brown hands I've held since then are descended from hers.

That fall I stopped in Laurelton, where I hadn't been since the previous winter. One evening my mother cornered me, whispering, "Daddy said not to wear pants on the train."

This was surprising—my father had never issued rules or instructions.

"It isn't nice," my mother said.

Then she went to join my father and I went to the room

where I was staying, which had been my sister's and had a canopy bed with a ruffle and matching spread. The threaded ribbons in this room were blue. There was also a chintz chaise. What was mine was my first phonograph, a heavy wooden box with innards, a graduation present. Like my new, free, adult life, it had been with me all summer. I put on a record I'd just bought in the city—*Wanda Landowska Plays Bach*—and lay on the chaise and looked at the ruffles. My parents knew I was on my way to the city; I had written them a long, careful letter outlining my plans; I was twenty-one and legal; still I didn't want to hurt them.

Next morning my mother told me that staying alone in my room wasn't nice either. I was to sit with them in the evening, she said. This time she didn't say who was requesting.

But when I left she gave me a mattress, and the gooseneck lamp that had lit my nights at the piano; and though she hadn't taught me to cook she brought out some pots from the back of the pantry. Still I sensed that neither of my parents believed this person I'd become; I think they always blamed me on the *goyim*. Perhaps they saw me as that, now. To avoid alerting the neighbors, I guess, they drove me to Manhattan at night, the two of them pale and solemn under the naked mattress roped to the roof of the Chrysler. This was October 1955.

Center for Mass Communication (CMC) was the grand title of a small film library with offices and a projection room in a second-floor storefront loft on Amsterdam Avenue. I was hired there as a clerk and then went on to write "promotional literature," at a weekly salary of forty-five dollars, three tuition credits at Columbia (to which CMC belonged), and long friendly lunch hours of bread, cheese, wine, and *Nanook of the North*. Knowing nothing of film I jumped right in, and felt very important running downtown to the Forty-second Street library to do research for my boss, Eric Barnaow. Evenings I went to the Thalia to see old flicks, or to Cinema 16, the Off Broadway of the movies, to see not flicks but films like *Un Chien Andalou.*

School itself was less educational. The playwriting teacher gave me an A and told me my stuff was "bold and original." But what was original in fictitious scenes—using what was *not* in the book—for an adaptation of *Daisy Miller?* Then I was asked to work an opening night at the Brander Matthews Theater. I arrived to find the crew all astir: with two hours till curtain, the king, in a student-authored fantasy, was minus half his clothes. The costumer had failed to send the pants.

I studied the action, the worried faces. Why were these people wringing their hands? Didn't they know the show must go on? "Do you have fabric, a machine?" I asked. "We do we do!" they cried, and then stood about in wonder as I measured, cut, and sewed. The show went on; the pants lasted; I split.

Linda and I lived with two other women, one of whom, to declare she was gay, hung a lipstick-stained bra from her light cord. Myself I was happy to be in the world with men. One of Linda's teachers played trumpet with the Red Onion Jazz Band, and we began to hang out at their *gigs,* a word I learned with other hip signals like *later.* Dick Hadlock played slide trombone with the band; he'd just bought the *Record Changer,* a magazine with ties to "traditional" or "Dixieland" jazz, the kind of music the Red Onions attempted. I went to bed with the band's banjo, a pretty drifter younger than I, with whom I was happy until original sin came between us. One day he said, "Let's get in our nudies and do *dirties.*"

Then he took me, in his red MG, to meet his family in Albany. "You can sleep with the Jew but never marry her," his father told him. Marriage was not on my mind but I was

16

offended and soon unfaithful. The banjo found solace in Linda. Things got sticky. One night I opened the door on them, and was struck by their perfect physical match. *Goyim*, I thought. That shamed me. I went to a meeting of the Jewish group Hillel, but all I saw there were people unlike me. Summer arrived. I read Whitman in Riverside Park at night and watched the mighty Hudson's march to the sea. I dated a Pakistani, an African who lived at International House, and a Jewish-Lutheran lawyer from Washington Heights. Among a group of a hundred and fifty, I took a class with the well-known scholar Eric Bentley, on the theater of Brecht. Although Brecht had succeeded Lorca in my affections, I couldn't stand the class. "I expect a working knowledge of German," said Eric Bentley from his faraway lectern. This isn't theater, I thought.

Not long afterward, my job at CMC was defunded and Dick Hadlock offered me part-time work at the *Record Changer*. Only a dollar an hour, he said, but it might be fun. Dick was a fair, generous, soft-spoken man with an interest in history, a little older and more experienced than I. He owned a 1927 Rolls-Royce and wore a chauffeur's cap and preppy glasses. "Come downtown," he said, "you'll like the Village."

Seven Morton Street, #20, had white brick walls and Manhattan's smallest bathtub, and was listed in the new, twelve-page *Village Voice* as "semiprofessional and semifurnished." The semiprofessional got me excited, and the furniture was fine because I didn't have any. I moved in, on New Year's morning 1957, with the mattress, the gooseneck lamp and the phonograph, and the pots I never used. A few days later my parents gave me the kitchen table they were throwing away. I went out to Queens to help them and we hauled it into the city on top of the car. My father kept sucking his teeth. Then he balked at the stairs. "Five flights," he complained. "Ach, for what? Why live like this?"

A good question that, the first and only time he ever asked. It was also my parents' last visit. Every so often I took the train to Laurelton, and sat with them in the evening, but each time that life seemed farther away, as Virginia also quickly receded, and even my recent year at Columbia. Only the present seemed crucial, only the Village seemed real. Coming back in the morning rush from Queens I'd be heartened to see Manhattan through the railroad's dirty windows, and feel myself drawn closer and closer to all that now was dear to me and familiar.

MORTON STREET

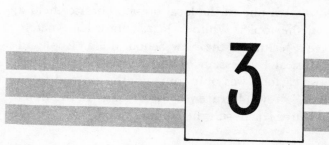

3

True to its pun of a name, the *Record Changer* had been published, since 1944, for collectors of records like the ones stuffed into Dick Hadlock's store. These people bought and sold the fragile, tinny history of jazz, all yet to be reissued on unbreakable LPs. Sometimes, concerned as they were with the artifact, they acted as if jazz had already happened, that the real thing was only on wax. We called them "moldy figs." Along with lists of collections for sale, the *Changer* featured essays, reviews, and interviews. Folk and jazz music were often interconnected studies. All these collectors and essayists were white.

The new, critical question seemed to be what jazz *was*, since it tended to change, as from hot to swing to bop to cool, and was all threaded through with the blues, which also would not bow to definition. To call jazz Negro music meant whites couldn't play it and they wanted to; to call it Negro music also put on it what was put on Negroes themselves, and no one wanted *that*. Part and parcel of every discussion was sociopolitical theory, and the history of racism, and, whatever jazz was, it was on people's minds. The week I moved downtown one of the local branch libraries held a discussion on the topic "Whither Jazz," the critic Anatole Broyard gave a lecture at the New School titled "Cool and Hot Jazz—Musical Expression of the Zeitgeist," and Jules Feiffer, whose cartoon was only four months old and titled "Sick Sick Sick," drew a lecturer saying of jazz, "If you don't like it you'd better learn—it's the coming thing."

Working with people can tell you a lot. I liked the pleasantly dependable nature of the *Changer*'s new Shipping Manager, whom Dick had hired—sans interview—because he was clearly overqualified for mailing records, and seemed like a person you could spend half the day with. Myself I'd never had trouble working, and I recognized the ethic in him, it was part of his mental health to lope in every day in his hurry-up, headfirst way. For his dollar an hour he put in his time. With patience and intelligence, in good humor about the close quarters. He even *typed*. And the way he pronounced his name, with a short *e*, as in e*le*mentary, *Le*Roi, struck me less as pretense than correction—at least it was half the way you said it in French. Anyway the short *e* emphasized the second half, and that's what he told us to call him—Roi. Roi Jones.

In the crowded store on Sullivan Street there was always room for one more stack of records or another visitor squatting on the steps that led to Dick's bedroom. People dropped in all the time, flung their coats on the shipping table, and sat down to talk. Work stopped; on went the phonograph, and then came the illustrated lecture—snatches of solos, bridges, riffs played over and over. The first critic I got to know was tall, grinning, gracious Martin Williams, subsequently director of the Smithsonian's Jazz Program, who was always natty and slick, in a belted raincoat, like a private eye with a baby face. He and Dick were the first white men I met who didn't make me feel uneasy. One day Martin arrived with a handsome young man with Boston broad *a*'s and a dark, affirmative beard, a friend of his named Nat Hentoff, who sat on Dick's messy desk all afternoon, swinging his legs and yelling "But you *caan't* say that!" Nat had recently written a piece for the *Chicago Review*, accusing American intellectuals of overlooking jazz "as a musical language and a way of life." He and Martin would soon publish a magazine of their own, *The Jazz Review*. To them there was no one "real jazz," because like all art it was subject to change without notice, and their objective, in writing of it, was less to debate its absolute form than to consider it part of a wider arena. They called it a uniquely American art form, thus predicting a new approach to black culture, as well as an even more significant economics: live people require live money—*you dig.*

Any seminar worth its salt develops one's critical sense. I discovered mine had an edge of impatience with picky distinctions that missed the point: the music. Also this long romance with "Negro life," or "way of life," troubled me. After the shacks I'd seen in the South I refused to link hard life with art; at least I wasn't convinced that the latter required the former. To me the hard part was simply to jump the wall, to do the thing at all. I was having trouble—my poems were awful, I thought. But I basked in the genial, nonconformist air at the *Changer*, and shared the assurance that something would become of us all . . . eventually. There was a guy around the Village then named Jean Shepherd, who had an all-night radio show and was the host at various events. That spring of 1957 he wrote that he'd been speaking to artists in widely different fields, all of whom felt that America was "on the edge of some sort of cultural swell."

My own metaphors weren't as ambitious or mixed as Mr. Shepherd's but I knew the feeling well. Besides the Jewish-Lutheran lawyer I was seeing a photographer, who had just bought a motor scooter, a hot item then. We used to go for amazingly bumpy rides on the East River Drive. All over the city there were ads for Vespa scooters: the driver was absent but the passenger was wearing a tight skirt and had been posed on the bike sidesaddle, smiling, though the smallest pothole would have bounced her off and killed her. Compared to hers my life was real and risky, with open, straddling thighs, and wild rides through the sea-laden air of the magical New York night—whoo! I regret, now, not having the tongue then to tell of it.

One day the Morton Street landlord called to say that the semifurnishings—the two canvas chairs, the bullfight posters, the slotted spoons, and the mirror—were all mine to keep. I hung up alarmed, part of me in rebellion, as if one thing could lead to another, and acquisition portend settlement, a hidden domestic agenda.

Anyway I wasn't using the chairs much, or the kitchen. Most often when I was home I sat in front of the shallow fireplace, burning vegetable crates from the Bleecker Street markets, eating Wheat Chex and worrying about my future. I had just read William Carlos Williams, concluding that my own poems were not only bad but worthless. I missed the small, easy challenge of CMC's "promotional literature." Because what—or who—was the subject of Morton Street? My single-minded coming of age lacked conflict, I thought. If, as Aristotle claimed, the plot was the soul of the action, what was mine? What could be said of me? That I'd managed to get where I was? And where was that? Dick suggested I keep a journal. I wrote small impressions, likes and dislikes, about wanting to live unencumbered by things. I made a list of the men I'd slept with, to see if I could shock myself (I couldn't).

Ruth Grossman, Dick Hadlock's fiancée, was a tall, talky children's librarian who laughed a lot and never seemed indecisive. She'd usually stop at the *Changer* after work, striding into the store like a bohemian Mary Poppins and shouting out "Good evening, Mr. Hadlock!" Her family lived on Washington Square, and her father, the economist William L. Grossman, had done the first English translations of the Brazilian novelist Machado de Assis. Dr. Grossman also wrote about jazz. Ruth's sister, like mine, lived in New Jersey; mine was a housewife with two small children, hers was an animal trainer. The Grossmans were a revelation to me; their two generations seemed to share a reality; I felt privileged just to witness such lives.

I laid my writing problem in Ruth's lap. I'd done children's theater in Virginia and had thought about writing for children. She urged me to try; at her job in Brooklyn, she said, the books for kids were old and dated. We agreed that this was important work—and unregarded.

But where in my fast new world did fairy tales fit?

I'm backstage on Christopher Street, at the Theater de Lys (now the Lucille Lortel). Low ceiling, hot lights, old wood smelling of greasepaint and nerves. It's the end of March 1957. Having failed to write a line for a week, I've returned to work in the theater. I've arranged, through a friend at Columbia, an appointment with a stage manager here. Out front is *The Threepenny Opera*—Brecht at last!

But the stage manager, a young man, is noncommittal about a job. "Let's get out of here," he says at the end of the act. We take a cab to his place on Avenue C. At once he attempts to drag me to bed, and puts me out when I refuse. Avenue C is deserted, a two-mile walk from Morton Street.

Cabs don't cruise there. I don't care. All the way home my proud, pinched face floats like a ghost past every little storefront.

Seven years after my encounter with him, this man would direct the premier production of two plays by LeRoi Jones, the *Record Changer*'s Shipping Manager.

I never had "normal" fifties plans—they seemed preposterous. Then one wet April night my lawyer friend laid it out: "Don't kid yourself," he said, "the Village is okay now, but you'll end up in Mamaroneck with Marjorie Morningstar, wait and see."

I was shaken by that. I thought Marjorie, of Herman Wouk's novel, had given up her life before she'd tried it. Everyone I knew had read and dismissed her; Hollywood had already made the movie on location in the Village. We were sitting, the lawyer and I, at a stained marble table in the Rienzi, a café on MacDougal Street not far from the alley where the movie had been shot. It was late. Various pale habitués stared through the rain-streaked windows, as if waiting out some crisis along with the weather. In contrast the ruddy-faced lawyer was firmly assured, with a handlebar mustache. I admired him. Though he was poor he had all the graces. He'd arranged for a rich friend to buy me my first meal of frog's legs.

I looked at him now with my mind a blank, as close to fear as I'd come, unable to summon a single vision of myself as suburban matron. People had warned me, but no one had ever presumed to predict me. What did he know that I didn't? What unforeseen catastrophe would send me up the river to decorate a home in Westchester?

My motor-scooter man had a loft on Ferry Street, overlooking the Fulton Fish Market, where hardly anyone lived then. Whenever this wheel I had my shoulder to seemed stuck, usually around three in the morning, I'd take the subway downtown and wander through lower Manhattan toward his place. I liked scuffling through Wall Street's left-over paper. Once a patrol car trailed me, then cut me off in a narrow pass called Theater Alley. A wary cop leaned out the window. "Do you know where you're going?" he said.

"Sure," I said, smiling at the irony, since I was only where I was because I wasn't sure at all. But the idea, as I saw it, was to ease the possible past the expected, and in this eerie solitude, while the rest of the world was home in bed, I'd feel closer to the edge, the spillover point that might push out something, make the coming move clear. What should I do now to make myself happen? What's next?

The door is open on a spring afternoon. Dick is out soliciting ads. Roi and I are minding the store. He's typing labels. He's fast. "Where'd you get so speedy?" I ask.

"In the Air Force."

He'd told us he'd been to Howard, but this was the first I'd heard about the Air Force. I ask him more questions; he replies easily, he likes to talk, he's all energy, the exaggerated V of his hairline goes up and down like a signal. "I was stationed in Puerto Rico," he says, still typing. He stops and looks at me. "In the Strategic Air Command, but they threw me out," he says offhandedly, and when I ask why he says, "for reading the *Partisan Review*."

Researching my thesis I'd read some issues of *Partisan*, the leading intellectual journal of the thirties and forties. Even in these Cold War fifties, it shocks me to think that his life was so changed by the same inquiry. "My god," I say.

He shrugs and goes back to typing, bent over the keys in his neat green button-down shirt.

Dick and Roi and I are mailing out magazines and talking about our families. "Lower middle class," I say. "Hopelessly

27

middle class," says Dick. "Much more middle class," says Roi. He's got a roll of packing tape in his hand and he gestures with it to make his point.

"The Negro middle class is a bunch of imitation ofays," he says. Then he turns to me for some reason. "You need to read about that. A good book just came out, E. Franklin Frazier, *The Black Bourgeoisie*."

I nod seriously. I know nothing about any of this.

It's one of those crowded afternoons at the *Changer*. The photographer Bob Parent has been to a Pentecostal church and his glossies are spread out on all the available surfaces. Martin Williams is sitting on the steps to the back room. He and Roi are talking about the bassist Charlie Mingus, who has the first downtown jazz workshop. Roi and Martin have become friends. They agree, then disagree, then burst out laughing. "That's not what we said in Newark," Roi says, and the way he says the word, *Nourk*, is exactly the way I remember my cousins saying it.

"Did you go to Barringer High School?" I ask.

He whirls around. "How did you know that name?" he says.

I'm alone in the store. Dick and Roi have taken Dick's dog for a walk. Suddenly they burst in bent over laughing. The dog is bounding around.

"That *dawg*," gasps Roi. "This surly wino was asking us for money and—he he he! *He he he!*"

"Peed on the guy's *crutch*!" yells Dick, and the two of them collapse again. "HE HE HE *HE HE!*"

It's a gentle May evening, with a faraway light blue sky. A bunch of us are hanging out on the sidewalk in front of the store. Roi's friends—among them his girlfriend—have come to pick him up. Someone tells the story of a girl whose friends refused to believe she'd sat down to eat with a Negro.

"Jesus!" says Roi's girlfriend in disgust. She's a gray-haired woman, full of complicated political opinion. I'm impressed by her hair as well as her points of view. All my politics, to my chagrin, exists in a cloud above my head called justice. But wasn't art about change, as my teacher had said? Why had Roi himself spent the winter in a cold-water flat with his feet in the oven, trying to write?

"LeRoi," I say, teasing. "The King."

"Yeah, the king," he says, self-deprecating. But something says he would wear a crown if he had to. The spirit in his dark eyes shines. We stand there, under the arc of a new moon, joking and laughing and liberated, we assume, from all that has gone before us.

Apartment 20 gets morning sun and I'm soaking it up in the window, on the wide sill, eating the first peach of the season. I've got a snatch view of the corner market on Bleecker, where the peach comes from and where an old Italian lady who likes me is setting out more of them. When I buy things from her she pats me and adds extra to the bag, and when I protest she says, "You too little already."

I'm too lazy to write in my journal, neglected beside me on the sill. I gaze at the scene with all its old, dusty charm. I've got a terrible case of spring fever. I've given up the unbelieving lawyer. Sometimes I go for midnight rides with my Ferry Street friend on his scooter. I might go back to the theater. Nothing's happened but something will, I'm as blind certain as ever about the future. Looking back to the street I see the peaches, glowing in the sun. On my way to the *Changer*, I think, I'll stop and buy some. They'll be warm and I'll pass them around. Roi said he likes fruit.

It was mid-July—watermelon weather—the day we got together. At the *Changer* we were working late, and even with the door open it was hot. I grumbled something about wishing I had my watermelon. Thanks to my friend in the market I had a huge piece at home.

Roi, who was working with his back to me, stopped what he was doing and glanced around. "You have watermelon at your house?" He sounded surprised.

"What!" I said. "Jews aren't entitled?"

He's laughing. "Dig this," he says. "When I was at Howard I got reprimanded for eating watermelon near the highway."

"You're kidding," I say, shocked, and reach across to pass him another order. And there—all at once different in the same green shirt—is the lean, inviting back of a lovely young man. I let my hand rest, let the feeling diffuse. Then I say, "Well—you want some watermelon?"

There's such pleasure on his laughing face as he turns to accept.

Half the night we sat up reading Shakespeare, both of us shy to make a move, the way it is, sometimes, when the person beside you is not some stranger with suddenly unsettled blood but someone more vulnerable, already more than face value, a friend. But we kept inching closer together over the book as we read aloud various parts in the plays, and finally we just sort of fell across the pages and grabbed at each other, and then move we did, the earth and all. We used to joke about that watermelon.

We spent that one night. Roi seemed as surprised as I. In the faint, early light I came awake to his embrace, and later he whispered, so sweet and shy, "Do you remember this morning?"

The next day I went to Newport, Rhode Island, to sell *Record Changers* at the Third Annual Jazz Festival. I jumped off the bus, pinned my press pass to my sundress like a medal, and went to look. The outdoor, out-of-town music fest was still a new idea, a new use for country ball parks. Under the weathered wood grandstand at Newport was a huge door posted PRESS AND PERFORMERS ONLY. I was trying to haul it open when all at once it flew toward me, bearing with it Miles Davis, in an Italian summer suit of lightweight fabric that American men were not yet wearing. "Hey baby," he said. And oh that cloth!

But most of the weekend I sat—listening to Miles and Louis Armstrong and Billie Holiday and Mahalia Jackson among others—far from the outfield bandstand, at a table in the catcher's cage near the entrance, selling magazines to whomever I could catch.

With my mind not far from New York, and me afraid I'd already made it up. I didn't understand the suddenness of the attraction—it *wasn't* there until it *was*—but I couldn't continue something this strong, I felt, unless I was ready for more. I liked Roi too much to trifle with him.

In a piece written many years later, he described his own decision as "going for that, for the difference it made."

I was a lot more concerned with this difference.

At Newport I stayed in a boardinghouse, in a bare, narrow room with semiglossed walls that reflected the moon. I wrote in my journal: "How will Laurelton take this?"

Then I lay wide awake on the neat little army cot, pressed down by thought. Just before dawn a couple next door made love, with zest, on a bed with squeaky springs. Their breathy rhythm invaded mine until I became insubstantial, as if isolated in my heart. The air in the room was almost the sea itself. I'd never felt so lonely.

I hitched a ride home with some of Dick's friends. In the car was another young woman, the wife of a critic, a few years older than I and certainly out in the world longer. On the way we made a pit stop, at a house in Connecticut, where the dining-room floor had been painted white and then dribbled over with color, like a painting by Jackson Pollock.

31

I was staring at the floor, trying to determine what about the real Pollocks made them so much better, when I first noticed this other young woman's high-heeled mules. She was wearing these with tight toreador pants, a style that keeps coming back like a song and has always served the same purpose.

In contrast were my demure old brown sundress, the bulk of my new handmade sandals. I thought again of the young man I'd left in New York. For whom I wasn't a fantasy, unbalanced and encased, but a woman who'd just begun to make her own self up. A man who knew I was weird, whose own hopes I respected, and in whose arms I wanted to be. The perfect mate for me—and here I was dawdling! So what if there might be "complications," what a crock that was! We could handle them! We could handle anything, I thought fuzzily, didn't we already run an office?

Relieved, I fell into a dead sleep as soon as I got home. Next morning I went out early, intending to comb the streets until Roi turned up; I expected to have to go all the way crosstown, looking in the park or the coffeehouses; I'd even decided to stop at the *Changer* to see if I could find the address of his place on East Third Street, where I'd never been. But there he was—unbelievably only two blocks away— walking toward me! He was with another guy who immediately said good-bye and left us standing there, right in front of Greenwich House. I felt as if I were grinning all over myself, mostly because he was too, as if we'd both been wound up the same amount, like two clocks. "Where are you going?" he asked.

"I was looking for you," I admitted before I could stop myself, and then, embarrassed, looked down at the sidewalk. You were never supposed to say that to a man, least of all one you were falling in love with, but I was so glad to see him I couldn't pretend. He just laughed, though, and I laughed too, and we went to have breakfast. I never did know where *he* was going that morning.

The jazz that was the coming thing arrived that year at various downtown locations—Max Gordon's Vanguard on Sheridan Square in the heart of the old Village; the Half Note among the misty commercial streets of the Lower West Side; and on the East Side, the direction Roi and I took most often, in a bar reclaimed from the skids at the head of the Bowery on Cooper Square. For eighty years the Third Avenue El had blocked the sky there; now it was gone, leaving a space that looked surprised by its size, as if waiting for something new to fill it. The address of the small, low-ceilinged bar was 5 Cooper Square; the owners, two brothers named Termini, called it the Five Spot. In the summer of 1957 the composer-pianist Thelonious Monk was playing a long engagement. When you opened the door the music rushed out, like a flood of color onto the street.

Monk's chords explained to me, finally, why I'd always looked for the *wrong* notes on the piano. Every night I heard a new sound, or heard sound a new way. And I suddenly knew a score of new people—some of them Roi's friends from Newark—the trombonist Grachan Moncur, saxophonist Wayne Shorter and his trumpeter brother Allen, drummer Tom Perry, who read John Stuart Mill and died of drugs. There were so many more, a long list, including the master inventor Monk himself, carrying a furled umbrella, and then laughing at us when we gasped as he pulled out a sword! I remember a whole lot of laughter at the Five Spot. You can hear it on all the recordings made there. I think of us trying to laugh off the fifties, the pall of the Cold War, the nuclear fallout—right then, the papers were full of it—raining death on test sites in Nevada. I think we were trying to shake the time. Shake it off, shake it up, shake it down. A shakedown.

In the United States white people have historically made their way to places like the Five Spot in times like the late fifties—New Orleans, St. Louis, Chicago all had their scenes, whites went to the Harlem Renaissance, too. But it's important to the particular history of what would later be called the New Bohemia that going to the Five Spot was not like taking the A train to Harlem. Downtown was everyone's new place. The cafés were hosting new poetry, there were new abstract expressionist paintings in a row of storefront galleries on East Tenth Street, new plays in new nook-and-cranny theaters—one of them, the Sullivan Street, in a basement up the block from the *Changer*. The jazz clubs were there among all of this. And all of us there—black and white—were strangers at first.

Black/white was still a slippery division to me. In Laurelton the rabbi had said Jews were a different people, but my schoolmate Mulligan's priest assured her that I was another race. The South had only served up reinforcement, and by 1957 I'd had little counterexperience. It would be two years before Philip Roth's Neil Klugman (in *Goodbye, Columbus*) described himself—with some difficulty—as "dark."

Music was my first written language—I read notes before words—and it had also come coded. In school, during World War II, we sang "I Am An American—Shout Wherever You May Be!" I knew America was the only place in the world where Jews weren't dead, but I didn't *feel* American; American was the Top 40s, and the Grand Ole Opry on the radio, the *goyische* Mozart and Chopin I played. It wasn't the Latin dance instructor who came with his records to our Laurelton basement—*Ola! La rhumba, cha cha cha, merengue!* And it most certainly wasn't those ancient, non-Western tones I loved to push through my nose: *Boruch atau adonai elohaynu melech haolum*. . . . My family, who went to the synagogue once a year, called me *rebbitzen* (rabbi's wife). But I'd learned Hebrew only to sing it, and what I'd wanted to be—girls couldn't, until 1987—was a cantor, a *chazen*.

However, I entered the Five Spot, and all these other new doors I opened with Roi, as another image—one-half of the blackman/whitewoman couple, that stereotype of lady and stud. This was unsettling. Despite having been to school in the South—or maybe because of it—I was amazingly naïve about interracial sex. Separate bed, separate entrance, it was all the same to me. I didn't even have a full lexicon—I'd never come across the word *buck*, for instance. That summer *Dissent* magazine published Norman Mailer's essay "The White Negro." There I read that jazz was orgasm, which only blacks had figured out, and that white "hipsters" like me were attracted to the black world's sexy, existential violence. But the only violence I'd ever encountered, the one time I'd heard bone smashing bone, had been among whites in the South. The young black musicians I met didn't differ from other aspiring artists. And jazz music was complicated, technically the most interesting I'd heard, the hardest to play. All I wanted to do at the Five Spot was *listen*.

Grachan Moncur told me I was the first white girl he'd ever met who came for the music and not for the kicks.

One night, after the last set was over, someone—not Monk himself—began to play "Greensleeves" on the piano. He played tentatively at first, and then, as the harmonies settled, with chords that took the simple line into an elegant statement, a hymn. I guess he just took us to church, as people say, but this was more than the gospel I'd heard, or Mahalia Jackson at Newport, and I'd never felt this way outside a synagogue. A hush fell over the emptying club, and on either side of me spaces opened, and I could see the same feeling in all of us, at once both apart and together, absorbing the clear, absolute notes.

From then on I never bothered with attitudes. It seemed as if another, new, language had been offered me, as old as the spirit I felt in myself, a music I could trust.

For those who still don't believe it, race disappears in the house—in the bathroom, under the covers, in the bedbugs in your common mattress, in the morning sleep in your eyes. It was a joke to us, that we were anything more than just the two of us together. We called the black/white lesbians next door "the interracial couple."

Still there's a certain kind of outdoor life when you're playing the other *Romeo and Juliet,* the one where nobody dies and hatred lurks, phantomlike, in every face except the most familiar, and can at any time become overt.

One moment stays in my mind. We were walking, early evening, along Bleecker Street, arm in arm. The catcalls began and continued. There weren't a half-dozen steady interracial couples in the Village. In 1950 thirty states still had miscegenation laws. I'd never even thought about that. When I understood that the jeers were for us, I turned.

Ready to fight or preach, whatever my inexperience required. Nobody called *me* names.

But just as quickly Roi grabbed my arm again and pulled me around. Not violently, yet with an urgency I felt right away.

"Keep walking," he said. "Just keep on walking."

It was his tone that made me give in, and only later that I realized we might have been hurt, or *killed*—and him more likely—had we been out of New York City. My ignorance embarrassed me. The dangers became more obvious. Also, and most important, to live like this I would have to defer to his judgment.

This gave me some pause. I am not by nature obedient. I began to have moments when I felt we ought not to mess up each other's lives. I knew my family would be troublesome. Mostly I was haunted by the problem of remaining a Jew, but I didn't know how to reinvent a Jewish woman who wasn't a Jewish wife. "I think I am losing my Jewishness," I wrote in my journal, and then, "Grr . . . what is that?"

I looked up all my old boyfriends. I ran away one night with the motor-scooter man from Ferry Street. Roi wrote his first poem to me then, about how badly I'd treated him. I wept and was so contrite. Then he showed me a poem about "dancing" with another woman, one night while "his wife" was away. That was some relief, at least both of us were guilty.

But certainties always come down to me when I am not looking them up. Catching the sun one mid-September afternoon, I was sitting on the shallow step to the *Changer* with my knees drawn up under the wide skirt of my dress, and a copy of *Measure* magazine balanced on them. Roi always brought me books, or magazines of new writing such as this—Morton Street was littered with the latest and my head was full of it. All at once, intent on *Measure*, I took exception to something in a poem I was reading—about a man and a woman, written by a woman—and the very thought process, once begun, evoked such pleasure of illumination, such certainty about the opposite view I held— Well, *I'll* always be my *own* self is what I thought—that I leaned against the doorjamb, enraptured and full of the sun. Just then Roi came out, and slipped a hand over my head, and said, in his charming, word-playing way, "What's happening, McVappening?"

But when I turned to return the ball ("Whatdya mean, jelly bean?") I was still too enthralled with my vision to speak, so with one hand I held up the magazine, and with the other I pulled his fingers down to cover my face.

And then I grinned at him from behind his own hand.

And, at that moment, as he appeared to me in all his dapper, young, familiar self, all my last doubts disappeared. At the Five Spot the music had spoken, and now here were the words. The signs were clear. I would follow the language with this man, and find the tunes.

Soon after, at a party, I remet the critic's wife, the woman with whom I'd come home from Newport. She went on— and on!—about how different I seemed. I assured her that I was exactly the same, that only the season had changed, but I knew what she meant. There's nothing like love to make you look good. All the guests at the party had gathered in a circle, the host was Armenian, and we were doing a traditional Armenian dance. I was wearing my gray-green fedora with the peacock feather in the band, and new red Footsaver shoes. I probably had on long earrings, too. I was clapping and dancing and laughing and having a wonderful time.

"Now *she's* Armenian!" our host cried, pointing at me.

And Roi and I fell out laughing, in that way people would come to know and remember us, heads close, bodies leaning into one another, tight as ticks.

By then it had become so natural for us to be together that I didn't realize how obvious it was to others.

One Saturday, after a visit to Laurelton, my parents gave me a ride to the *Changer*. They were late and drove quickly away with only a wave at my welcomers.

Next visit my mother popped the question. "Who was that Negro boy?" she asked.

"My friend Roi," I said. "He works there too."

"Next thing you know you'll be living with him," she said.

I didn't answer. She was kneeling at the foot of the stairway, pinning a hem for me. I looked down at her round back, her mouth full of pins. I felt sorry that there'd be stress, as I knew there would be, about Roi. But I didn't feel compelled to discuss my affairs with my mother. I never had, and now I'd been away from home for nearly seven years, long enough, it's said, for all the cells of the body to change. My life with Roi was still a precious, new thing. I wasn't ready to give it away.

Not so my companion. One Sunday Roi woke up and decided he needed a haircut, and since his father was the family barber he called Newark and said we'd be over. An hour later, six blocks from my aunt's apartment, I stood, feeling near, far, shy, and hungry, on the Joneses' front porch. They had the first floor of a large frame two-family. The tree-lined street reminded me of Brooklyn.

It was Mr. Jones who answered the door. Slender as his son, he bent a gray head toward us paternally, and said, "Have some breakfast!" in one of those deep voices you normally find in a larger man, a very different tone from Roi's but full of the same confidence. He didn't seem in the least surprised to see me and neither did his wife, who was standing balanced back on her heels with her hands jammed in her skirt pockets. Her prematurely gray hair was exactly like her husband's; they were a matched pair, a set: he was a postman who was also a champion bowler—on the dining-room wall were shelves of trophies—and she was a social worker who'd been a runner (her own medals undisplayed, although she'd once been the second fastest woman in the world).

They'd just moved to this apartment, it was new to Roi. I realized as his parents showed us around that I'd been right to think of Brooklyn. The layout here was exactly that of the first home I remembered—the three steps to the cellar, the wide kitchen in back. All of a sudden I felt six years old.

While the haircut went on I helped Mrs. Jones make breakfast. She worked for the Newark Housing Authority. She'd been to Tuskegee and Fisk University. Roi resembled her. "How nice," she said, "that the two of you have similar interests."

He'd been right, I thought. His family *was* more middle-class than mine, better educated and worldlier. Actually, he could have patronized me.

"You know I wasn't here when Roi called, I was in a meeting at the Y," Mrs. Jones said. "But his father said he was bringing someone he wanted us to meet, so I came home." She smiled.

In a flood of relief I smiled back. She was telling me how much she loved her son. I knew she would understand—and appreciate—my own feelings for him. And I would tell her, when I knew her better, that I also liked to stand, like she did, with my hands in my pockets. My own mother had cautioned me against it—you'll stretch out your clothes, she'd said—but that was the stance, I thought, of a woman who stood her ground, a woman who'd take a stand.

Later that afternoon, Roi and I played softball with some of his high-school friends. I pitched, lefty me, and struck someone out. The pride on his face!

I thought about pride that night, back on Morton Street,

with him asleep so peacefully close on the narrow bed. I was proud of him too—his quirky intelligence, his good humor, his stride. He was the first man I'd ever met who never failed to engage me. He was funny. He was even-tempered, easy, kind, responsible, and everyone else liked him too—I thought he was such a good *catch*! How I would have liked to show him off, to bring him out one Sunday on the railroad, to a Laurelton that might have shared my pleasure in him. But all I had to offer was this self of mine, in its alienation, behind me the burden of closed minds. There was a sad, dull fact to this, with ridiculous ironies. Because if I was the one who kept watermelon, it was Roi who loved a good sour pickle.

It's a sunny late September morning on Morton Street. We're hanging around, reading the paper. Roi's in a chair, one of the two the landlord said I might keep, and which, were we your typical fifties couple, we would now think of as "our furniture." Except we never think about furniture. Like money, it's simply what you come across. Luckily, we don't think much about food either—except the dollar salad at Café San Remo, split between the two of us, with lots of free bread and butter. (I haven't learned to cook.)

But we're living on love, of course. Last night we went to an Ionesco play, *The Bald Soprano*, and laughed louder than anyone else in the audience. That's another thing I like about us—we make noise. We play. He jumps over fire hydrants and tries to vault parking meters, eek. I whistle in the street, and tell him how my mother used to tell me to stop that. And when I am my usual antic self, the look of pleasure on him is like grace. With no effort, or adjustment, I can't imagine life without him.

And there's a way we approach the fact of our being together that has none of the high seriousness the world seems to wish on it. Little Rock, Arkansas, has just refused to integrate its schools. Federal troops were called. But nothing touches *us*; people stop and stare and we sail on— what else should we do, fall on our knees and ask their permission? Sometimes I still want to toss my head or stick out my tongue or shriek *We are not illegal* but I have learned, and I am learning every day.

Today I'm sprawled on the bed, thinking about what to do next. I've just finished reading the new, hot book *On the Road*. I love Jack Kerouac's footloose heroes, who've upset complacent America simply by driving through it! I don't know whether Roi and I are among "the mad ones, the ones who are mad to live, mad to talk, mad to be saved," but I know I don't want to go on the road right now, not while New York is the best place in the world. Nothing could tempt me away.

Though nagging my peace is the fact that Dick's dollar an hour is not enough anymore. Besides, he's running out of money himself and is thinking of closing the *Changer* and moving to California. I heave an elaborate sigh, a shoo-in for attention.

"What's the matter?" Roi comes up out of the *Book Review*.

"Hand me the want ads," I say gloomily.

He smiles at my terrible expression, but he'll be out of work soon too. "I'll read them," he offers.

I smile at him. How generous. But I don't hold much hope. I'll never find a job that's anything like the one at the *Record Changer*. It's probably back to the straight world for me. But where? What? And I don't *want* to. "Lots of luck," I say to Roi, and bury my face in the magazine.

Then in a few minutes he says, "Hey, look at this," and I hear disbelief. "Look at this," he says again. "*Partisan Review* wants a subscription manager."

"*Partisan Review!*" I jump off the bed. "Stop teasing me,"

I mutter, and crash down beside him, poking pages out of the way. "Let me see."

And, indeed, there it is. "Well, *I'm* a subscription manager," I say, incredulous. And then we're all over each other, laughing. But we remember to save the ad and the phone number.

The next day William Phillips, one of the editors, had nearly the same reaction. "You're really a subscription manager?" he asked. It must have seemed unlikely, not the kind of specialization expected from a drama major. But he was impressed by the fact that I'd done film research for Eric Barnaow at Columbia. (I didn't tell him I'd done that *once*.)

"And you *know* the magazine," he said doubtfully.

"Know *Partisan*? Why, of course," I said. "A friend of mine was discharged from the Air Force for reading it!"

This seemed to reassure William Phillips, who hired me on the spot. I left in a hazy euphoria. Eighty dollars a week and all those words! I couldn't imagine anything better, anything more thrilling—and the two, cluttered, scruffy rooms on Union Square confirmed all my rebellious suspicions. Here was real upward mobility—plus I got my job through *The New York Times*! What a joke!

Running downtown to spread the news, I caught my wide grin in Fifth Avenue's windows, above that same brown dress I'd worn home from Newport. And I'd been hired in my old clothes! Was it my direct eye, my innocent confidence? I'm curious now, I never thought of *why* then. The world was my oyster, that's all. And the pearls! . . .

Those two rooms were soon what the ads called a "one-girl office," since added to subscriptions were also "all phases magazine management." With literary quarterlies, international journals, *Dissent, Midstream, Hudson, Poetry, Kenyon, Encounter*, the London *Times*—and books, books! An ocean of words and opinion surrounded me like the jiffy bag fuzz I'd scatter each morning in my rush to open the mail.

And as Union Square was familiar, I preferred to hole up, noon hours, in the grimy-windowed *Partisan* office, with a peanut butter and jelly sandwich and whatever I happened to be reading.

In a very short time I discovered myself barely educated, with great intellectual gaps where everyone else had stored movements and cultures. What had I learned at Mary Washington—Roi called it my "teacup college"—except an illusion of independence from the men who called the shots? "That's the trouble with you young people today, no sense of history!" William would yell cheerfully, shaking his finger at me. Yet he was always kindly instructive, and I liked watching him edit, the care for the precise word, the very generosity of honing another person's argument. When I began to take charge of business with the printer, and there were times when a line here or there had to be saved, we would spread out the proofs and go over them. The content dissolved in the pleasure of sweet manipulation.

Still my mind balked at the academic focus on criticism, the same texts run over and over like obligatory laps. I imagined the nine letters of N.e.w. C.r.i.t.i.c. as the nine Supreme Court justices, presiding over all that was robed and respectable. And Moby-Dick, solid and impenetrable, with all these critics sliding down his sides. I knew William was right but sometimes I felt defensive, as if it were only *his* history he thought I should know. Where was the guide to my situation, cultural or political—where was my life in all these pages? I felt, as always, that I had no precedent. Except—to give credit where it's certainly due—the time William said to me, with a terrible look of astonishment: "What! You've never read Tillie Olsen!"

Fortunately, neither an acceptable Moby-Dick analysis, nor an enlightened Lenin approach, is much to the point in running a magazine, even a literary one, and with a sly acuity of eye and ear I could fudge it. The past regretted, I had no complaints about my present education. William's co-editor, the critic Philip Rahv, also seemed to trust me and like William was willing to teach.

"Copyedit this," he said to me one day, putting a manuscript into my hand.

"But I've never . . . How do you do it?" I said.

He hesitated, frowning, then patted my shoulder. "Just make it right," he said reassuringly. "And change it from English to American."

That I felt I could do. By luck I had grammar by ear, and knowing American was high on my list. What I didn't tell Philip, or William—not just yet—was that I thought we were defining American now, we of the "misalliance," we of the new world, the one that hadn't yet livened their pages.

The Mills Hotel, on Bleecker Street at Thompson, was a dank, cavernous, derelict's roost and occasional home to desperate artists. On the Thompson Street side it had a narrow café, which opened for a time as a coffeehouse called Jazz on the Wagon. Although the music was only occasional, and the place was funky and hastily constructed of plywood and the floor slanted, a small but provocative literary group sometimes gathered at the squeezed-up, wobbly tables. They even had a name—the "Beats"—ambiguous enough to include anyone.

Jack Kerouac had thought up "the Beat Generation," in conversation with another writer, John Clellon Holmes, who later explained *beat* as "pushed up against the wall of oneself." At the readings at the Wagon—and the Gaslight, Limelight, Figaro and other Village cafés—not all the poetry beat the agony. Roi and I were almost too sane in a group where shrink-time seemed mandatory. To be beat you needed a B-movie graininess, a saintly disaffection, a wild head of hair and a beard like the poet Tuli Kupferberg, or a look of provocative angst like Jack Micheline. Ted Joans was another beat picture, a black man always dressed in black, from a black beret on down. The women, like me, had all found Goldin Dance Supply on Eighth Street, where dirt-defying, indestructible tights could be bought—made only for dancers then and only in black—which freed you from fragile nylon stockings and the cold, unreliable, metal clips of a garter belt. The Beats *looked* okay to me, and I applauded their efforts, successful or not, to burst wide open—like the abstract expressionist painters had—the image of what could be (rightly) said.

Public readings were a new, qualitatively different route for writers. Few were in print and performance counted— how you sound, as Roi said. Besides Kerouac, the other beat hero-poet was Allen Ginsberg, whose *Howl And Other Poems*— published in San Francisco, in the fall of 1956, by Lawrence Ferlinghetti's City Lights Bookshop—had been seized by Customs and the police and tried for obscenity. (It won.) Roi got Allen's address in Paris and wrote him, on toilet paper, asking if he was "for real." Allen was pleased and responded. Roi was asked to read his own work. Soon we'd met the poets Gregory Corso, Diane Di Prima, and then Frank O'Hara, who was also a curator and took us to the Cedar Tavern to meet the Tenth Street painters—Larry Rivers and Alfred Leslie are the first of those I remember but soon I recognized more than a few and picked them out of the crowd at the Five Spot, where they also were regulars. At the Cedar we met many of the artists who'd studied and lived at Black Mountain College, the legendary home of avant-garde education, which had just closed. The days went by in a streak of events and performances. John Coltrane succeeded Monk as a main attraction. Atlantic Records advertised "the label in tune with the Beat Generation." In England a current play was described as a "soap opera of the Beat Generation, British version." One dark, jammed night at Jazz on the Wagon Roi and I were introduced to the suddenly famous Kerouac himself, a medium-sized, rather shy man. Critics had called him "a voice," but he seemed bewildered by the ardent young crowd for whom he'd spoken.

That fall, after the Russians sent up *Sputnik*, the world's first spacecraft, the suffix "nik" was added to beat, putting us square in the enemy camp. There was some humor—Ted Joans and photographer Fred McDarrah rented themselves to parties as "genuine beatniks," dressed appropriately and carrying a set of bongos, an instant symbol for Negro culture. Although like hipsters the Beats appreciated jazz, they weren't content to leave it where it had always been left—in its "place." Jack Kerouac's "spontaneous bop prosody," for instance, was an attempt to sophisticate the English language rhythmically, to make it *work*, like music. Like the writing of Martin Williams and Nat Hentoff, this did prefigure a different approach to black culture, and got on some literary nerves:

"Oh, man! man! man!" moaned Dean [in *On the Road*]. ". . . here we are at last going east together. . . . Sal, think of it, we'll dig Denver together and see what everybody's doing although that matters little to us, the point being that we know what IT is and we know TIME and we know that everything is really FINE. . . . Listen! Listen! . . . He was poking me furiously in the ribs to understand. I tried my wildest best. Bing, bang, it was all Yes! Yes! Yes! . . ."

It was only a ten-minute walk from the *Partisan* office to the Village hubbub. I brought what I'd learned, and judged Roi front line. Not just for love: I'd read enough to see that his voice was unique. He didn't use a lot of words, but then again he didn't have to. Sometimes, like Miles Davis says about notes, you just have to play the pretty ones. Roi wrote what he knew, from a fresh point of view. Onstage he was clear, musical, tough. He delivered.

He was also looking around for another job while finishing up at the *Changer*. Usually I met him there after work. One evening when I arrived he was on the phone. While he listened he kept gesturing at me and slapping his forehead. Then he said, "Yes, I'm well aware that he's a Negro, but he's been a fine employee. He hasn't stolen anything, if that's what you mean."

I gaped at him.

"We'd be glad to vouch," he said pleasantly, but with an expression that was new to me. His jaw muscles jumped, repeatedly and noticeably, as if he were gnashing his teeth while the rest of his face remained calm. It was a look I would come to know.

And this was the story: a record collector he'd seen about a job had just called the *Changer* to ask for a recommendation. Dick wasn't in. Thinking to get himself hired, Roi had pretended to be someone else.

Of course we laughed. But it brought home how suspect he was, simply being his competent self. Like, though so *un*like, most of our new friends. Yet often what was said about them applied to him most: "The freaks are fascinating," wrote one critic, "although they are hardly part of our lives."

My own life still worried me a little. Beside my desk at *Partisan* I kept a big green metal waste can, where most of my lunchtime attempts to write got filed. I was too ashamed to show them. I didn't like my tone of voice, the twist of my tongue. At the open readings, where anyone could stand up, I remained in the cheering audience. Roi was so much better; everyone else was so much better. Only one poem I wrote then survives, a sort-of-but-not-too haiku.

Nevertheless I didn't feel down for the count. All the Beats found it funny that I worked for the *Partisan* titans.

Sometimes I hired Diane Di Prima, who had become a friend, to stuff envelopes and keep me company. I was able to bring Roi books and magazines. And at *Partisan* I could already see a stir of reaction, a gearing-up of the generations. William was considering poems by Allen Ginsberg and Gregory Corso. I felt happy to have landed—by remarkable, marvelous chance—in the middle.

But it was slick little Roi himself who made me feel most needed and wanted and appreciated, and it didn't seem (though this would change) that he loved me any less for my silence. But I did begin learning how to cook. My first pot of brown rice was inedible—a gummy off-tan mush. The two of us, hungry, stood peering into the pot in the little corner air-shaft kitchen on Morton Street. "What'd you do?" he said. "I don't know," I said. Still I felt nothing but hope in the future.

night   sky

     sleep   lover

        one,   two,   three

     lights—

in the city

5

On Morton Street the fireplace was less for ambience than for late-night warmth. Evenings I'd run ahead of the garbage trucks to pick up vegetable crates, or I'd get them from the woman at the market. She'd seen me with various men, I guess, and one evening she held me at arm's length and gave me a long, hard stare. "Do not," she said, "sleep with those earrings on. You'll get pregnant."

I laughed and tugged at my ears, where long, elaborate curios dangled, nicely incongruent below my androgynous hair. And I might have taken her advice, because—out of irresponsibility and ignorance—I wasn't doing anything else besides watching the moon. Which up to that time had worked. Two of my former roommates had been "caught," as we said. But of course it wouldn't happen to me.

So it must have been the earrings. The symptoms were confusing, a week or two passed before I figured them out. When I told Roi, he—the responsible one—took me to his family doctor in Newark. Diagnosis confirmed.

I'd given no thought at all to having a child, never dreamed of babies—I wasn't yet done bringing up myself. There was no way in the world I could have this baby. That it would be an "interracial" child was only secondary, though this surely was there too.

Roi seemed hurt and angry when we talked. Although he never clearly said so, I was sure he thought it was only *his* kid I didn't want, and that ultimately I wasn't the "wife" of his poems. But the decision as well as the fault, I felt, was mine. Through a friend I made an appointment with Dr. Spencer, who practiced in Pennsylvania and periodically went to jail for saving some of us from death by coat hanger. Legend had it that he'd lost a daughter to a botched abortion.

It was winter when I went, by myself, to the small town with its one street and horizon of iced-over hills. "You've come alone?" said the nurse sharply. "Yes, *ma'am*," I said, angry to find my independence shamed. I couldn't have risked Roi's presence, even if we'd been safe outside New York; it was enough to take with me, all those miles, the sight of his bent head when I'd left him at the bus station. I spent the night in an old brown hotel, talking to him on the phone and reading a Gideon Bible.

The next afternoon, still a bit drugged, I was waiting at the side of the road for the bus to New York when a car came along and slowed as it passed, and a man shouted, "Oh, you must have been a *bad girl!*"

At home I resolved to reassure Roi that I loved him, and to consider how I felt about having "interracial" children. Could a white mother raise them? And white I would be, because I knew the Jews—mine at least—would give me up. But letting the matter rest seemed the only solution. I looked, with a fresh eye, at women with children. I knew I'd know what to do when I did it.

After a while Roi understood my position; without pressing, he took me on faith. That spring he wrote a poem in which he referred to me again as his wife, and declared, among other warm sentiments, that I would one day have a child the image of his "rogue-faced" father. I carried a copy of it in my wallet.

Recovered, wearing a Woolworth rhinestone wedding ring, I went sensibly to the Margaret Sanger clinic for a diaphragm. They made you insert the slippery, unfamiliar thing yourself, after one demonstration, from a recumbent position, with only a mirror at the far end of the table for a guide. ("Feel that? Like the end of your nose? That's the cervix—get behind it!")

Afterward I was asked to be part of a survey. Cohen was the name on the check I was writing. "Race?" asked the interviewer. I looked up. "Race of your husband, Mrs. Cohen?" she asked. "White?"

There in her poised assumption lay my challenge, and all the decision I would ever need went solid as a rock in my heart. "Negro," I said.

She glanced, with a slight frown, at the check that said Cohen.

"He was . . . adopted," I whispered.

Our magazine—*Yugen, a new consciousness in arts and letters*—was Roi's idea, but, as he's written, I "went for it." I think I threw myself at it, actually. Few magazines out of New York, to that date, had promised the new consciousness that everyone downtown agreed was just what the world needed. I know mine was raised by the very act of press-typing each quarter-inch character of that *new consciousness in arts and letters*.

We rented a rickety IBM with erratic adjustable spacing, and rigged up a light box for pasteups; Roi collected poems and drawings—among the contributors Allen Ginsberg himself and the artist Tomi Ungerer; Dick Hadlock offered production advice; even the motor-scooter man from Ferry Street helped with graphics. Piece by piece I put it all together, on my old kitchen table, with a triangle and T-square borrowed from the *Changer*. Finally, 7 Morton Street, #20, was semiprofessional!

Yugen 1 was neat, twenty-four pages, serious looking, its cover print an ochre on off-white grainy paper, the white spaces making the face of a man you don't see at first because he's in reverse. His own eyes aren't focused either, he seems to be looking wildly at the ideogram running across the cover in front of him, the Japanese character for *Yugen*, which I drew, and which means, as the title page noted, "elegance, beauty, grace, transcendence of these things, and also nothing at all."

At *Partisan* I'd had pleasant business dealings with the distributor Bernhard DeBoer and his wife, who took on *Yugen* as a favor and helped to put it into otherwise inaccessible places, like Midwest campus libraries. Roi and I went to the DeBoers' in suburban New Jersey for lunch one muddy spring Sunday, and they photographed us. We both look silly and not at all beat in our old straight clothes on a couch in front of a sunburst clock. And this was our distinct advantage: self-sufficient, self-propelled, we could go anywhere we were invited.

We set up everything right for our new enterprise, solicited ads, kept careful accounts in a cash book I bought ($1.29, February 26). On March 3 we paid the printer, in a couple of weeks I recorded the first sales—$10! And on page 3 of the April 2, 1958, *Voice,* in a box so you'd notice, *Yugen* was announced as a "New Quarterly on the Stands."

There were times I'd unexpectedly come upon that mustardy cover, with its ideogram like a little action painting, and my eye would claim it again the way you do with something loved and familiar. If I hadn't yet managed to speak for myself, here at least were these others. The first poem you come across, opening *Yugen* 1, is "Further Notice" by Philip Whalen:

> *I can't live in this world*
> *And I refuse to kill myself*
> *Or let you kill me*
>
> *The dill-plant lives, the airplane*
> *My alarm-clock, this ink*
> *I won't go away*
>
> *I shall be myself—*
> *Free, a genius, an embarrassment*
> *Like the Indian, the buffalo*
>
> *Like Yellowstone National Park.*

We threw our first party to celebrate *Yugen.* A&M Beer Distributors got twenty-two dollars for a keg, but the person who gave us the empty loft hadn't paid Con Ed. Halfway through the night the lights went off. We rushed to the local bodega for candles. Then we lost sight of each other.

And I wasn't looking for Roi, nor he for me I'm sure, when long past midnight all at once we came face to face. Something flashed in his eyes, a passion—not only of love but *recognition,* to which my whole being responded. We fell together and seized each other, as if we'd been apart for months. As if this happy bash of people were only another thing we could do, another result of our easy collusion,

another love knot. As it was. We were both twenty-three
years old. I thought there'd be no stopping us.

The Spring 1958 issue of *Partisan* included "The Know-
Nothing Bohemians," a book review by Norman Podhoretz
that was an elaborate trash of *On the Road* and disparaged
the rest of the now officially Beat Generation.

Podhoretz was angry, mistrustful, and self-congratula-
tory. Although the same age as Kerouac, he feared and
loathed what he saw as our degeneracy and anti-intellec-
tualism: "The spirit of hipsterism and the Beat Generation
strikes me as the same spirit which animates the young
savages in leather jackets who have been running amok in
the last few years with their switch blades and zip guns." He
felt that this gang would surely destroy America's literary
future. And he was outright insulting, I thought, referring
to "dispossessed urban groups (Negroes, bums, whores)."

Almost everyone I knew was disturbed by the essay, Roi
especially. I ventured this opinion to William, and offered
him a rebuttal, although he'd already assigned one to someone else. "I'll get you a really good one," I said.

"You will?" William seemed dubious. How could there
by any worthwhile writer he didn't know?

"Oh, I will, you'll see," I assured him.

Roi wrote what I thought was an excellent letter, showing off his considerable knowledge of literary history and
quoting all the right names, like Randall Jarrell and Robert
Lowell; he defended *On the Road* and *Howl*, reminding that
the work itself, not its structure, was at issue: "To write a
novel in bop language is not the point, no more than it was
Shakespeare's *point* to write his plays in Elizabethan English."
He maintained that American literature needed new life: "If
one thinks the hipster's language meaningless, perhaps it is
not entirely the hipster's fault. . . . The point is that the

56

language can be extended and enlivened by just such prosody as Kerouac's. . . ."

The Spring issue of *Partisan* had also featured two essays on the Negro writer in America, by Ralph Ellison and Stanley Edgar Hyman. The separateness of black life, its culture seen as a "folk art," was a subject Roi also wanted to address. Podhoretz had said that bohemia was, for the Negro, "a means of entry into the white world," and that no Negro bohemian would "cooperate in the attempt to identify him with Harlem." "Harlem," Roi replied, "is today the veritable capital city of the Black Bourgeoisie. The Negro bohemian's flight from Harlem is not a flight from the world of color but the flight of any would-be bohemian from what Mr. Podhoretz himself calls the 'provinciality, philistinism and moral hypocrisy of American life.' "

When I brought William the essay, I watched as he looked it over with his quick editorial eye. "Hey, this guy's a *writer!*" he said. "Sure we'll print this!" Then he looked at me curiously, and smiled. "Your boyfriend, huh?" he said.

The next issue of *Partisan* had poems by Frank O'Hara and Denise Levertov, two friends whose work I admired, and also Delmore Schwartz, an old favorite of the editors who had come to the office early one morning lonely and disheveled, and had stayed to talk. It was his dramatic criticism that led me originally to find *Partisan* in the Mary Washington College library. I told Delmore this, and thanked him, and he, first of his generation to want to be seen with us, promised me a poem for *Yugen*. But then he died.

THE BEAT GENERATION, AN EXCHANGE, appeared in capital letters in a box on the cover. Below the title, Roi's name was dead center. Inside, on the masthead, I had become the "Advertising and Circulation Manager."

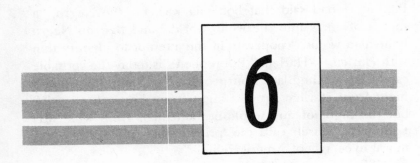

Billie Holiday, whom I very much admired, only lived long enough to be on TV twice. The night of her second appearance found me in Laurelton, visiting. I hadn't been there since May and now it was July, and hot, and good to be out of the city. My father was away fishing and my mother had invited me to dinner, in celebration of my twenty-fourth birthday the week before.

I lay on the living-room rug close to the set when Billie came on. "Isn't she incredible?" I said to my mother, who was behind me on the couch reading *Life*.

"Love is like a faucet," Billie sang. "It turns off and on."

"So what does that mean?" said my mother with a scowl. "Like a faucet? How stupid."

I turned back to Billie and the other musicians. Even distanced by the medium, they seemed closer than my mother. Why did she pretend to know so little of love, after all her Broadway plays? How could I ever expect her to understand Roi? In May I'd brought her a copy of *Yugen*. She'd riffled through it with a vague "That's nice," and made no further comment. At dinner tonight, apropos of my birthday, she'd warned, "You're getting old—twenty-four is almost thirty." I knew what this meant: unmarried women my age were pushing their luck. But I couldn't explain Billie's blues—or the life I'd chosen—until my mother was ready for life as it was.

"Love is like a faucet," Billie sang. "It turns off and on." The shadows crossed her face as she sang. Myself I didn't want Billie's hard life, but only her genius approach to craft. I've written about her since—the more you know of her voice, the more there is to admire. I wanted a tone like that, like a sure bell, and to sing like her ahead of the beat, on my own line, in my own good time.

This was, as my mother might have said, a tall order. Another was confiding in my mother. I'd seen different, more conscious bonds between mothers and daughters: Ruth Grossman and her mother, Roi's mother and his sister Elaine. But you couldn't, magically, set them up all at once, and I wasn't my mother's mother, although I felt like that at times.

But if I was ahead of my mother that evening, Billie was long past me. "Love is like a faucet," she sang. "It turns off and on. Sometimes when you think it's on, baby, it has turned off and gone."

In his 1927 Rolls-Royce, Dick Hadlock once drove to Harlem wearing a chauffeur's cap, with Roi, *le roi*, lounging on the high backseat. On a hot August Sunday a few weeks after I'd seen my mother, I rode in the Rolls with Dick and Ruth to the Great South Bay (Long Island) Jazz Festival.

It was good to see the musicians off their usual cramped,

hot stages, out in the fresh air. Charlie Mingus, in a bright Hawaiian shirt, like a flower bent over his bass, and Miles Davis, pressing out his muted notes, sharp in a summer suit—even at the beach! And all of us under a flapping tent, with the moving sea and some little white boats in the background.

I listened to a set or two in the tent and then went off alone to the water. It felt good just to sit in the sun, among families. I was tired—I slept as little as I could, of course, in order to have more time, and the self-indulgence of life-as-art sometimes wearied me. There was a little black boy nearby, there on the beach, having a time with his ball, his mom (white), and his dad. I suddenly realized that nothing but my own capability had been in question. Not whether to have an "interracial" child—that was irrelevant, the child would be black. One-half, as Roi always reminded, makes you whole. Which left only the personal: could I? All I foresaw that lovely summer day was ease, a little life, thriving. It could be done. Look at this one here. The little boy rolled his beach ball to me, and I rolled it back, and the problem rolled out on the tide.

Partisan gave me a paid vacation in August. I flew to Boston to visit a friend from college who'd just given birth to her second child. During the night the baby woke. Thinking to give my friend a break, I found a bottle in the fridge and warmed it. I'd never even fed a baby, so uninterested had I been. Never imagined a small, earnest, working face in the stillness, the way it fit against my breast. Thunder and lightning! Not only *could* I, but oh, did I *want* to! And *would* I! And I'd better hurry, too, hadn't my mother said I'd soon be thirty? I didn't think I had to ask Roi, I felt I had his permission. I didn't think about how this decision might affect my own ambitions. I simply saw that little mystery, and fell for it.

With utmost ease I became careless about what I called

my rubber-baby-buggy-bumper. I forgot to pack it when we went to Long Island at the end of the summer to spend a weekend with *Yugen* contributor George Stade and his wife, Dolly. It rained but we had a good time anyway; we went to that classic creepy movie *The Fly* ("Help me! Help me!"), Roi spent a patient evening trying to teach me contract bridge, which I promptly forgot, and at night, stifling giggles at the cling of nylon tricot sheets, we fell into the hole in the middle of the unfamiliar bed and made a baby.

"I guess we'll have to get married, then," he said when I told him. We were walking down Eighth Street in the early fall twilight, and that sly little smile on his face was all I ever needed. He made the arrangements, hired the Buddhist Temple, found a doctor for the syph tests, and bought me a jade ring. This was it, we were now to be official.

My sister's husband, Paul Fenichel, whose stubborn devotion to her I'd always admired, agreed to intercede with my family. Before it all happened, though, Hettie Roberta Cohen would have to make one last visit to Laurelton. That it had to be *Yom Kippur* eve, a time of confession, I took as a sign and a test, and got on the railroad.

It's warm for late September, I don't mind my bare arms, or the thin crepe of my chemise, already the only dress that still fits. Beside me my father's hands, dark and thick-nailed, rest on the open *machzor*, the liturgy. My mother's at his right, with rouged cheeks and powdered nose. As usual I feel older than both of them.

Actually I'm twenty-four going on a hundred. I look down at my vanished waist and acknowledge once more the presence of someone I can't sort out from the beat of my heart. But this is the last service, I remind myself, the last *Kol Nidre* I'll ever be able to sing here. On the pulpit stands the rabbi, my onetime teacher. In a few months we'll meet, in a car outside the Theological Seminary (no place in the building, no room at the inn). He'll tell me the baby's color is of no concern to him. As long as it's a Jew, he'll say—and I won't believe him. (Years later, on the front page of *The New York Times*, he will be seen welcoming Anwar Sadat to America.)

But now in the Laurelton Jewish Center a breeze comes through the open stained-glass window. Open, the perfect design is spoiled, the autumn leaves outside are spotlighted, dancing and bright. I hear the sweet peace of crickets. That's what it's like for me, I think. Everything I want is outside.

But then I feel a chill on my arm, and now we've come to the reading of sins. I look down at the *machzor* for ones that apply to me. Here's one for arrogant mien, one for haughty eyes, for obdurate brow, I beg forgiveness. For the sin of breaking off the yoke, *v'al kulom eloha schlichos*—yes, that's the one—for being someone these people could not influence, or hold, forgive me, but this is America . . . sometimes you have to go on the road.

And on Monday, October 13, 1958, I couldn't wait to start out. I was the happiest and best-loved woman in New York. Willingly, and without a clue as to where this decision would take me, I got up early, put on my best leftover-from-college suit, and rode, with my smiling intended, on the subway to Ninety-fifth Street. Where, at 10 A.M., at the ear-splitting sound of a huge brass gong, and with a promise to remain cheerful (the only one I remember), I traded Hettie Cohen for Hettie Jones.

Then it was time for the conference with my father. I hadn't seen much of him recently. Like my mother he never spoke of himself. Sometime that year he'd "borrowed" the rest of my graduate school money, a legacy from my grandmother. "For the business," my mother had said, but hadn't mentioned that the business was bankrupt.

He was weeping on the phone when he gave me an address a few blocks north of *Partisan*. I went there during my lunch hour, climbing an old, unpainted flight of stairs into a dark office with one desk. He was still weeping when I arrived. He embraced then dropped me, then paced back and forth, tears falling from his eyes, his nose running. "You can't do it," he sobbed. "It'll kill your mother." He went on. He didn't ask me to sit down.

This was exactly what I'd known all along he would do —and that he'd stop at nothing but my agreement. I was ashamed. Of him, but more so of myself, for my inability to comfort him, or do more than just stand there and endure him.

Suddenly he stopped and confronted me. "Get a divorce!" he shouted. "I'll take you to Mexico! You'll have an abortion and get a divorce!"

A surge of obstinacy seized me—and then immediate regret. I *am* older than he is, I *must* try to understand. "No, Daddy," I said, gently.

"No *no!*" he shouted. "No *no!* We'll go to Mexico, get a divorce, you'll have an abortion. Run away!"—he began screaming—"Just the two of us . . . we'll run away to Mexico!"

I lost my patience then. "That's crazy!" I burst out. "What are you saying?"

"Get a divorce! Have an abortion!" he wailed and then he grabbed at me, but I tore myself loose and ran for the door. On the wide wooden stairs I heard him yelling my name and I tried to go faster but I didn't want to fall. I mustn't hurt the baby, I thought, I mustn't fall. . . .

"Hello, Mom?"

"Oh . . . Hettie." She cries a little, then she stops. "Why didn't you call me before?" she says.

"I was told never to call again."

There's a silence. I don't ask why she hasn't called me, I didn't expect that from her. "I spoke to the rabbi," she says.

"Oh?"

"He says I should think of you always as my child, so no matter what you've done you're still my child." She pauses, weeping.

I look around my office, at the paper clutter, the full shelves. The heat's on, the sun's in the window, I'm swollen with ideas and comfort and life. And now even my mother's allowed to claim me.

"Don't cry, Mom," I tell her. "I'm glad to talk to you, too. Please don't cry."

George and Dolly Stade had stood up at our wedding. A few weeks into this married life we decided to pool our money and rent an apartment we all could share. *Yugen* needed a room too, as it would soon have a sibling, Totem Press. We were going to publish small books—poetry mostly—by various new writers. The Stades were to be partners in the venture. George and Roi found a big place in Chelsea. The rent was nearly double that of Morton Street. All plans were made, deposit paid. Then Dolly's father gave them money *not* to live with us.

We went to Chelsea anyway. Moving the mattress, Roi and his friend Louis Smilovich, a fellow refugee from the Air Force, were attacked by a gang on Jane Street. Louis wound up in St. Vincent's Hospital. I went over to the projects on the Lower East Side to look for his sister and tell her what happened. I found her camped in a vacant apartment with her boyfriend and some of his friends. She put the matter in their hands. They backed me up against the stove. "Why'd your husband and Louis get jumped in the first place?" they asked. "Why couldn't your husband save Louis?" "What kind of a friend is that?" "What is he?" "What are you?" They're not smiling. "Jewish," I say, "he's not." "What is he?" "Protestant-American." I insist but they're not satisfied, that's not specific enough. "Better not be a nigger," one of them says. I stick to my story.

△ △ △

All I remember about leaving Morton Street is what I forgot there, a pretty little antique typewriter. I missed it, but I never went back for it; I felt I'd left the subject along with the place, and there was only a forward set to my head. One night, introducing me to someone, Frank O'Hara called me Hettie Cohen. "Her name is Jones now," Roi chided gently. I smiled and put my arm through his. It seemed sweet and sentimental that this pleased him.

Despite the shared name, there were different transformations awaiting us. He would remain, like any man of any race, exactly as he was, augmented. Whereas I, like few other women at that time, would first lose my past to share his, and then, with that eventually lost too, would become the person who speaks to you now. Which covered some ground, even though I've never lived far from Morton Street, and from this room where I write I look down, as if at the steps I took, at the corner where the Five Spot used to be.

TWENTIETH STREET

O ne windy late fall Friday just after we moved to Chelsea, Roi and I went out to hear Jack Kerouac read his poetry. Jack's life had so far led from working-class Lowell, Massachusetts, where he'd been a football star, past Columbia University, the Merchant Marine, Mexico, both coasts, two marriages, many liaisons, and a child he wouldn't acknowledge. In the year since *On the Road* he'd been celebritized, endlessly criticized, pressed for definitions of Beat. The attention hadn't helped. I didn't know him, and after our one brief meeting at Jazz on the Wagon I'd only caught glimpses of him haggard, drunk, and surrounded.

The reading was at a newly opened, out-of-the-way place, the Seven Arts Coffee Gallery, a second-floor storefront on Ninth Avenue in the forties, the transient neighborhood near the bus terminal. The audience, mostly friends, numbered only about thirty. Unexpectedly Jack was sober, all slicked down and lumberjacked up, an engineer scrubbed clean for the evening (on the West Coast he'd worked as a trainman). I decided I liked this good-looking, friendly man whom everyone loved and admired, and I certainly admired his work, so when the reading began I sat alone at a table up front to pay attention. He noticed. He kept catching my eye and reading to me, and he was marvelous: relaxed, confident, full of humor and passion—and he wanted the meaning *clear*. At the end we all stomped and whistled and clapped and cheered.

A crowd of thirty, thus inspired, needs a big enough place to party. Our new house was a straight mile downtown, just off Ninth Avenue, and we had nothing but party space to offer, so after the reading we just brought the audience home, to 402 West Twentieth Street, a once elegant six-room parlor facing the weatherbeaten brick of the Episcopal Seminary.

In the arrival melee of coats and drinks and glasses and ash trays, I caught some puzzled glances from Jack, who looked as if he couldn't place me, as if he'd read to me as an interested stranger, and only now had noticed the burgeoning rest of me. To whom was this pregnant woman attached? I saw him whisper the question to Allen, who pointed to Roi.

The connection seemed to please Jack enormously—his face lit in the strangest, gleaming little grin. The music was on and a few people were already dancing. Suddenly he ducked and wove his way through them—fast, as if in a scrimmage—to Roi, who was at the other end of the two adjoining front rooms. Then dragging bewildered Roi by the hand he maneuvered back to me and grabbed me too, and then, with amazing strength, he picked us both up at once—all 235 pounds of us, one in each arm like two embarrassed children—and held us there with an iron grip and wouldn't let go!

What a pleasure to meet this funny, visionary Jack, who appeared to have such sympathy in him, a sweetness similar to Roi's that I found attractive. Word got out and soon the party of thirty grew to fifty, and all night Jack kept running to me with different people: "I didn't remember who she was," he kept saying, "but she was listening so hard at the reading, she was really listening to me—she *understood* what I said!"

That Friday night party never ended. Soon we had a studio couch and a folding cot, one or two weekly boarders, twenty or more weekend regulars, occasional bashes for hundreds. Under these circumstances, being the one who understands can get you a rep for sufferance. The writer Hubert (Cubby) Selby, Jr., once said, to my surprise, "I always meant to apologize for those years we crashed all over you." But never having to manage alone made all the difference to me, as never having to go home alone—or always having a home to go to—made all the difference to them. Twentieth Street was a young time, a wild, wide-open, hot time, full of love and rage and heart and soul and jism. Like everyone else, I tried to get my share.

Billie Holiday had been at Jack's reading, or at least she was outside the Seven Arts in a car. It was the poet Joel Oppenheimer, bearded and bespectacled and wild-eyed as a young Trotsky, who approached her while the rest of us kept a respectful distance. In the darkness the turned-up collar of his black overcoat seemed all of a piece with his hair and beard, and he must have been a sight to Billie, whose mouth opened slightly in surprise when, leaning into the open window of the car, he said, with all his avant-garde elliptic-profundo: "Thanks, Lady. Just . . . thanks."

"Thanks?" Billie said. "For what?"

Connected to the two front rooms on Twentieth Street was a narrow kitchen with high, thickly painted cupboards, and over the sink an oversize window of sooty smoked glass. The vague shadow of a wall loomed up close, the brightest day came through dulled. But dead center, onto the window frame, Roi tacked a poem by Ron Loewinsohn, the opening work in *Watermelons*, the first book issued—in 1959—by our publishing company, Totem Press. The poem brings to the reader the act of the art itself. It begins

> *The thing made real by*
> *a sudden twist of the mind:*

and ends

> *. . . thunders into*
> *the consciousness*
> *in all its pure & beautiful*
> *absurdity,*
> *like a White Rhinoceros.*

I read those words at all hours, in all strained lights, always to see that rhinoceros snorting toward me. The poems *were* our lives. Basil King, the painter who did some *Yugen* and Totem covers, claimed the beast himself. He was walking with Ron in San Francisco, he said, when Ron said, "We need an image that'll knock 'em over." "Well," said Basil, "how about a white rhinoceros?" And then later, pleased and surprised: "Damn if he didn't just go home and *write* about it!"

Whatever its country of origin, the presence of that animal over my sink was due to my husband, the sort of gesture from him that I valued. There's a habit to putting your heart on the wall, to modes of domestic expression. The one we fell into was peaceful and playful.

Another Friday, midwinter 1959, about six on a bitter cold evening. I've just come home from work, in the big black sweater I wear buttoned over an unzipped skirt. Although I always know it's there, I don't *think* about the baby much, most of the time I'm just living my life with it in me. Anyway tonight's a more imminent birth—*Yugen 4*. Something like the baby, its cover will be black with a white abstraction. Over the years every last issue will be sold, it will become, to the book trade, "rare." But now it's only corrugated boxes of reams of paper fresh from the offset printer. I hear the scuffle as they're dragged past the outside doors. Then, with a great show of strength, and moans and exclamations, they're carried inside by three excited young men.

In the lead, fair of face and form, with a midwestern open mien, is the cover artist himself, designer of the Totem logo, Fielding Dawson, known as Fee. He's one of the Black Mountain crowd, a writer and a painter. His blue eyes sparkle, his cheeks are red from the cold. Right behind him, wearing a jaunty peaked cap, is Roi, whose nose is red too, right through the brown, and who drops his heavy box— *bang*—as the cap falls off his head and rolls to the feet of the third man, Max Finstein, who neatly sidesteps, drops the box he's carrying—*crash*—his own hat falls off. The timing's perfect. They're bent over laughing. They think they're the Marx Brothers! I have to applaud. Max is a slight, wise, amber-bearded poet from Boston, the first man I've ever watched iron his own shirts. He's living on our couch at the moment.

In retrospect the three of them seem like a sentiment, a bohemian version of an ad for Brotherhood Week. But there—in that room designed for middle-class life, our formal "front parlor" with its tiled hearth and bay of venetian blinds—they're real, available to me, and revealing. And they're having such fun! Proudly stamping their frozen feet and blowing on their poor bare knuckles. Max produces a pint of brandy. We drink to the birth. Roi slits the boxes with my X-acto knife.

From a quick first look at *Yugen 4* you'd say Beat, as the three Beat gurus—Kerouac, Corso, and Ginsberg—were represented. Except the "new consciousness in arts and letters" was more inclusive. Like Basil King, Joel Oppenheimer, and Fielding Dawson, the poets Robert Creeley, John Wieners, and Charles Olson were out of Black Mountain College, where Olson was the last rector. Frank O'Hara, like the painters he knew, was a poet of the "New York School." Gilbert Sorrentino lived in Brooklyn, Gary Snyder in Japan, Ray Bremser in a Trenton, New Jersey, prison.

Gravely we check all twenty-eight pages. The centerfold is printed sideways, per instructions. But some of the covers are not what they ought to be. Fee looks disappointed.

I glance at Roi, who'd rather be perfect. He's got that tight look at the jaw, but he's still leafing through the box. "Hey, look here, the rest are okay," he says reassuringly, his own relief a little bit hidden. That's just like him. Of them all, he's the smallest, youngest, and skinniest. But he takes charge; he's the editor.

And he spent time at the editor's desk—the *Record Changer*'s huge rolltop, left to us by Dick and Ruth when they married and moved. (People regularly sat on it, but Joel—one crowded weekend—was the only one who ever slept on it.)

Past the kitchen on Twentieth Street a long hall led to three more rooms. The desk and books filled one, our narrow bed another. As for the third—because I can see in my mind its sunny, dusty window, I can't see why I didn't put a desk of my own there, and at my back a door that shut me into myself so I would write. I didn't even know how much I needed this. The room stayed full of a printing press someone gave us, which never worked, while I worked in the public eye, in the room with the double door that led to the street. Before we could afford to leave printing to the professionals, I put together *Yugen 3–6*, and a couple of small books, on a drafting board propped on the kitchen table.

Meanwhile we'd attracted attention. In late 1958, the critic Gilbert Seldes remarked that even though he wasn't always "with" the poetry in *Yugen* he found in it a lot of *feeling*—his italics. It was this that all my late-night cutting, pasting, aligning, and retyping finally taught me—what comes from reading things over and over, taking apart and putting together, the heart of the matter, the way it feels.

And there goes the doorbell. First Joel, with a scarf up to his nose, squinting from a day at the print shop where he works. After him the Brooklyn contingent: Gilbert Sorrentino and his wife, Elsene, with Cubby Selby, who looks like a sailor in his watch cap and pea jacket; then Joe Early, an editor, his wife, Ann; their friend Larry Hellenberg, a sheet metal worker; poet Sam Abrams and his wife, Barbara; Basil King and his wife, Martha; and Tony Weinberger, later the author of *Max's Kansas City Stories*.

With all these mouths to feed I get lots of instruction. The mysterious kitchen has been more or less revealed. I own a seasoned iron pot and a wooden salad bowl I rub with garlic, and I've mastered the rudiments, mostly of other people's ethnic dishes—though I've yet to shape a matzoh ball, I can make gumbo with okra and also spaghetti for a hundred. That's what we're having tonight. All the Italians are over the sauce. Both sexes—each one a poverty gourmet. No onions is Elsene Sorrentino's theory. She has two children and from my view a world of expertise. "No self-respecting Sicilian . . ." scoffs her husband, a tall, handsome man with expressive gestures and grimaces. "My mother would *never*," he says, flinging his arms around. Elsene goes on cooking. I see it's all part of the big-life-poem: "With a knife in the kitchen / I cut / a tomato" ("A Fixture," Gilbert Sorrentino, *Yugen 4*).

Spoon in hand I glance at my husband the host, who doesn't cook. But he does clean up these parties: his specialty is mopping the floor. Meanwhile he's standing back to survey the scene. In the parlor Max and Fee are setting out stacks of pages that seem huge to me, at least a night's work. But I'm sure the job will be done, and carefully, and Roi is too. Accomplishment is the virtue of our life together. With a wide, satisfied grin, his chin tucked in and his arms folded tight across his chest, he's leaning against the wall that divides the rooms. It's as if he's trying to contain his pride, to keep it from bursting out of his body the way it has on his face. I know how he feels.

Midnight. We pass around a second wind, a vial of heart-shaped Dexedrines, the kind that look like Valentine candies and should say LOVE ME or I'M YOURS. Bottles line the floor at our feet, an unmistakable smell drifts down the hall. But drugs are expensive, their purchase and use are still risky, and we're for life over death. Even William Burroughs, whose writing is all about using, had warned in *Yugen 3*: "Stay away from Queens Plaza, son . . . Evil spot haunted by dicks screaming for dope fiend lover. . . ."

Three A.M. The last pages have been passed. The dozen of us has doubled, the couch and chairs are crowded, the room is alive with a din that satisfies every emptiness I've ever felt. I'm adding covers to the final collated folded stacks, then passing the completed copy to Max, who's taking a turn at the stapler. Joel and Roi are having an argument, something about Ezra Pound. I stop what I'm doing to watch. Ray Charles's "What'd I Say?" is on the box. Elsene and Cubby are dancing. Martha King, in a paradoxical reaction to the Dexies, has fallen asleep. Her husband glowers from under his kinky hair; he thinks his wife can't hang. Roi's making a point; he's got his funny finger out while holding a quart of ale and the oversize bottle makes him seem even smaller, more concentrated, a bantamweight fighter going jab, jab, jab jab jab. . . . Suddenly, the strongest it's ever been, the baby inside me turns and turns again—dancing to Ray Charles!—and the copy of *Yugen* in my hand falls open to the sideways printed centerfold, a brief, compelling vision, part of the wide lines of "The Chamber," by Michael McClure:

> *Matchflame of violet and flesh . . .*
> *. . . clear bright light.*
> *. . . stars outside.*
> *. . . long sounds of cars.*
>
> *. . . the huge reality of touch and love.*
>
> *. . . real as you are real whom I speak to.*

To me the homosexual life seemed the hardest and riskiest, almost certain to drive people crazy at some point. John Wieners stayed with us a while that year. He'd come east from California, and en route had lost his top front teeth. Embarrassed, smiling shyly behind his hand, he perched cautiously on our studio couch, a pale contrast to the bright Indian print spread. I admired not only his poems but the magazine *Measure*, which he'd founded. I told him so, and thought of telling him I liked his (shocking then) ponytail, but he was so bashful I hesitated even to mention it. How did one encourage such a soul?

In a world that denied their existence, I admired gay

men who could party. Frank O'Hara and his roommate Joe LeSueur had a loft opposite Grace Church and they often filled it with people, including many women, with whom they were always friendly and careful. I liked gay irreverence, and it was Allen Ginsberg and his lover Peter Orlovsky who starred in my all-time favorite Twentieth Street party. Ambitious, dedicated Allen was in his early thirties by then. His twenties hadn't been easy—from Paterson, New Jersey, to Columbia University, a forced season in Bellevue—but now he seemed used to himself, and like Roi and me he made his own rules. I was drawn to this social ease, to his warmth and his smarts, his matter-of-fact relationship with Peter. The two of them sometimes liked to get nude in the middle of a fully dressed room—Allen dark, balding, bespectacled, Peter with a blond brush of hair and pretty body. Complacent, superior, they would pose—they never even seemed cold!—challenging the rest of us to follow (no one ever did).

Among our few possessions was a hat collection—a collapsible top hat I'd bought in a junk store, a Moroccan fez, a Stetson, a derby, a sombrero with long, grassy streamers. One Saturday night—I don't know how it started—there was a wild competitive rush for hats. After the real ones were claimed we had to invent. When Joel got a pot Gil got the salad bowl, the rest of us followed with paper, shoes, hastily reconstructed clothing. Joe Early looked like a bulky Sikh with his jacket wound on his head, and the woman with Cubby Selby braided her stockings into her hair. When I noticed Allen and Peter, they were stark naked and in a huddle, whispering. Then suddenly they shooed everyone off the couch, and heaving it to their heads began to dance around the room with it, yelling *"Hat! Hat! Hat! Hat!"* A roar of laughter rose and then applause for the winners, and so they took a victory run, around the front parlor, with the bright bedspread flipping and flapping around their bare posteriors!

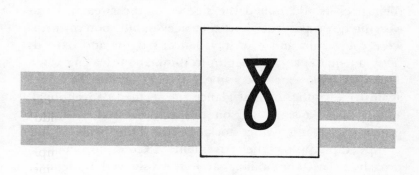

Back in 1957, when Roi and I were first together on Morton Street, I walked downtown from *Partisan* one evening to put up fliers for a reading he was giving. It was December, and blustery, not the kind of weather for managing paper and tape bare-handed. Also the sleeves of my coat—my "good" coat from college—were cut short, to the formal "glove length," a style that in my present life seemed shamefully impractical. I got to the Village ready to give up, with numb hands and wrists, and it was only because I'd promised Roi, who was at work cataloguing someone's record collection, that at Fourth Street I turned east instead of west and headed for the Five Spot.

The club was warm and quiet, and after I'd taped a flier

among the many on the wall, Joe Termini treated me to a brandy. Thus reinspired, I went up to Astor Place, and stood in front of Cooper Union, where I thought I could catch people coming out of the subway. But the wide, windy square wasn't an ideal location, and even the few homeward bound who looked bohemian rushed past me with their hands in their pockets. I'd pulled the sleeves of the sweater I was wearing down past the short coat sleeves, but soon my arms were cold again and even my dancer's tights and oxfords felt inadequate, and I'd begun to think about leaving when a woman about my age came hurrying across the street against the traffic. At first glance she seemed conventional, almost prim, a small person properly dressed in a neat princess coat and nylon stockings, the little heels of her pumps tap-tapping the pavement. Except, as she approached, a certain familiar carelessness showed in the mess of her flyaway blond hair, and then I thought I recognized her face, and just as she passed I placed her exactly: the woman who'd been with Kerouac when I'd met him at Jazz on the Wagon. So I chased her, and accosted her with a flier, and said hello because I could see she sort of remembered me, too, and I was just urging her to come to the reading when a sudden, icy blast of wind sent the two of us careening toward St. Marks Place. The air began to fill with snow. "My god," she gasped, "let's get *out* of here!" Grabbing my stuck-out sweater sleeve she began to pull me along, like a well-dressed nanny with a somewhat put-together child, and with the same authority, as if there were no question that I'd go wherever she was going without even knowing her. And since I'd met few women my age who seemed at least as determined as I, I took her at once for a kindred spirit, threw the rest of the fliers in my bag, and dashed off with her.

That evening we had coffee behind the steamy windows of the B&H Dairy on Second Avenue, where she introduced herself again as Joyce Glassman (years later, as Joyce Johnson—her first married name—she was to write several novels and the memoir *Minor Characters*). But when I was living on Twentieth Street, two winters after we'd met, she was still Joyce Glassman, and a good friend to me, and besides coffee we'd had knishes, and blintzes, and mushroom barley soup and potato pancakes, and any number of other treats in the B&H, Ratner's, Rappaport's, the Second Avenue Deli, and every other Lower East Side landmark. Joyce was a shopper, she knew all the little old-world places; we'd been to Essex Street's barrels for pickles, bought beans from barrels at Greenberg's on First Avenue. We liked Polish pirogi and Ukrainian scarves, and I liked Joyce because like me she took her independence for granted. Both of us were paying the rent. Neither of us had ever considered wanting a man to support us. And having sex hadn't made us *bad*.

Superficially, we were as different as our clothing that night on Astor Place. Joyce was a city girl, bookish, the closely watched only child of more ambitious Upper West Side parents. She'd been a stage child; she'd been to Barnard. But after early secret trips to the Village, at nineteen she'd left home with her stuff in a shopping cart, having fallen in with a group that included Allen Ginsberg, who'd fixed her up—a blind date—with Jack. That affair was over now; she lived alone on First Avenue, worked midtown in publishing. She thought I was lucky to be with Roi. But she was writing— a novel, already under contract—and that was her good fortune, I thought. We shared what was most important to us: common assumptions about our uncommon lives. We lived outside, as if. As if we were men? As if we were newer, freer versions of ourselves? There have always been women like us. Poverty, and self-support, is enough dominion.

In the eye of the Twentieth Street hurricane I found a big sister. Rena Rosequist was Joel Oppenheimer's wife then, the mother of two small boys, a lively North Carolina woman with a long blond braid always flying, grown from a nervy, athletic, intensely female-proud girl—the kind who drives a car at thirteen; "tomboy" would never describe her. One day in her eighteenth year she hitched to Black Mountain, with a friend who'd heard of the place. By then—the early fifties—it was a hothouse for avant-garde art, an experiment in community, home not only to writers but also composers, choreographers, painters, and sculptors. There was theater, too, even performances of works by Lorca and Brecht, and how jealous I was to hear that! Rena had studied drama too, at a nearby North Carolina college for women. She made her way back to Black Mountain again, eventually fell in love with Joel; her middle-class, Catholic family disapproved—a bearded, Jewish, Yankee poet! The morning Rena left home to be married, her mother stood in the doorway threatening suicide. The priest had been sent for. But Rena—amazingly nicknamed Sissy—slipped away before God's hand could stay her.

Becoming an artist's wife hadn't stopped her either. Rena held on to her own life, and she liked to keep women's minds on themselves. She'd stand with her hand on her hip and look down her nose.

"Heartburn!" I complained.

"The price you pay for eating a buttered English," she teased. "Watch your diet." "You must go to sleep." "Here, read this book." "Now read Adelle Davis." "Now go, right away, to New York Hospital—it's the *only* place in New York to have a baby."

The voice of experience was bossy, but I did everything it said.

Like most artists' wives, Rena worked. (In a midtown office then and has recently chaired the New Mexico Council on the Arts.) Working mothers were scarce then.

So was it man's, or woman's, world she gave me, the

day she handed me *Childbirth Without Fear*, by Dr. Grantly Dick Reed? It was one of those rare afternoons on Twentieth Street when all the men were out and we had the house to ourselves. Leafing through the book, the only one available then about natural childbirth, I found a description of the breathing Dr. Reed recommended. "Oh, that's easy!" I said to Rena. "I can do *that*—it's just diaphragmatic breathing."

"Diaphra*what*?" she said doubtfully.

"I learned how to do it at college," I explained, "in a course called 'Corrective Phys. Ed.' " I stood up to demonstrate, poking my belly under her nose. "See?" I said smartly, "in, out, in, out—diaphragmatic breathing."

"That's it!" Rena yelled, laughing, bested for once.

Later, alone, I read the description again, carefully, to be sure I wasn't just full of myself as usual. I remembered the day I'd learned the breathing, the sunny room, the hardwood floor, the classful of women taught by a woman, who had simply called it "a relaxation technique." Never hinted at—*why?*—was this possibility for its future use. Without Rena's help I might not have made the connection. It seemed as if the very life of our bodies was hidden. *By whom?*

My mother could tailor; she had solid skills, she could make slipcovers, and watching her I learned the machine. Sewing was also required curriculum at P.S. 156, where we girls took up bias binding, the French seam, and drawn-thread embroidery while the boys were in shop. Stitchery, though it paid less than carpentry, was nonetheless marketable. I spent my nineteenth summer making costumes, in a windowless shack in a children's camp high in the Adirondacks. I didn't like the place but I had no money, and nowhere else to go except home, where I'd vowed never to live again. Mornings I bent to my tasks like a starved, sackclothed apprentice, running silk seams for nobility. At night, to relieve the tedium, I walked two miles to the nearest inn and got drunk with the local timber.

Apart from the king's pants at Columbia, I hadn't sewed since. Until, too pregnant to wear an unzipped skirt and a sweater, I hauled out Grandma Sarah Cohen's Singer, and made two sensible jumpers from a pattern.

It was a quick seduction: the fabric, the eye-hand thrill, the color and shape and texture that are also the terms of music. The only drawback was the pattern, which I promptly discarded, as if throwing away the score, because to make it all up, to improvise, became a way—as Ron Loewinsohn's poem over my sink instructed—to "relate the darkness to a face / rather than / impose a face on the darkness." Or, as Roi wrote, "There cannot be anything I must *fit* the poem into. Everything must be made to fit into the poem." Or maybe, after all, sewing was just another excuse to put off writing, to find something else that plagued me less, and, as Djuna Barnes reminded: "One hides behind the hat with which one bows to the world."

Yet the lovely bravado of anti-clothing! And how simple to cut and fold large pieces, as in kimonos and djellabahs, the easy shapes found outside Western culture. You couldn't buy patterns then for "unconstructed" women's garments without set-in sleeves to restrict the arm and darts to shape—and reveal—the breast. But once you release the shoulder, and allow the breast its natural room, you make way for the next step, that of taking off the hard, restrictive bra (soon, soon).

So I think of getting to know my first child under a shirt that covers us both, me and the moving baby under white corduroy. On the fabric there were two wide stripes, black intertwined links, running from hem to shoulder up the back and down the front; in between the belly poked, as if cradled in suspenders. Zen-head that I was, I worried little

84

enough about that baby. I didn't have a doctor—I went to the New York Hospital clinic once a month. Dr. Spock seemed obvious, though I kept him around to consult for diseases. Besides—still catching up—I was reading *Ulysses*. But at the last party before that birth I had a run-in with one of the media-encouraged beatniks who had begun to swell the ranks. We'd made a strong impression on Al Aronowitz, a reporter for the *New York Post*. Though he liked us, Al really thought we were freaks. He came to all the parties and had just written "The Beat Generation," a two-week series with a daily front-page headline. We were hot. Everyone wanted to come take a look. What was it really like, life outside the vast conformist U.S.? A girl and I were in the kitchen, she in the fridge with the orange juice. The clinic had warned about Vitamin C. "Leave me some?" I said nicely, because I had no money for more. "Well!" she huffed. "I can see you're going to be one of those *professional* mothers!"

I was appalled.

But it wasn't just me I was pleasing. Much later, in the roar of music and dance, I'm standing with Rena when Roi, passing by, stops to rub the belly corduroy. *"That's my baby in there!"* he yells to Rena. And she, arch and affectionate, answers: *"Roi, I never doubted it for a minute!"*

But he also wrote that I was pregnant with *my* child, which hurt. I didn't understand that most men have such feelings, while their women alone know what's swinging between the suspenders. And his poems, like those of any honest person, also held moments of personal failure between us. Mainly he'd wanted the world to hear from me and it hadn't, at least not in terms of the going (male) intellectual positions. He liked my inventive clothes but where was my tongue? This had been part of his expectations. This was important to him. I should speak my mind. Why didn't I write criticism? "I / love you / & you hide yourself / in the shadows," he wrote.

Maybe the worst was the night he wrote "The Death of Nick Charles." (Was Nora, Nick's partner, ever pregnant? Did she work?) I'd come home from *Partisan* tired, made dinner, pushed aside the work I usually left on the table, and waited. . . .

Much later Roi came in and woke me. He had an essay by the French writer Antonin Artaud that someone had given him to publish, and he wanted me to get up and look at this coup. He was all excited. But he really wanted to boast about himself. "Everyone's talking about me," he said. "And my wife," he added, which I was sure he'd only said to temper me. I knew he'd been at the Cedar, where I couldn't be then, not while I was fat and tired and had to be home in bed. I suddenly saw how his life would be so different from mine from now on, and in an agony of regret I moved away from him, and turned my face to the wall. He got up and went to the typewriter. I could hear the sound of the keys but I couldn't move. In the poem he wrote, the agony is his:

> *To say*
> *I love you & cannot even recognize*
> *you . . .*

His own conflicts, some of his hidden need, surfaced the first time we were ever to be separated. A carful of poets, led by Allen Ginsberg, was going up to Gloucester, Massachusetts, to visit Charles Olson. Roi was pleased about the trip, as he'd never met the much-admired Olson, but he wasn't too happy, I don't think, about arriving with a mostly gay group. He'd once confessed to me some homosexual feelings, though never any specific experiences. Before they left we sat together on the passenger side of the front seat, waiting while everyone else got settled. Suddenly he grabbed me and clung, something he never did. I hugged him tight. Not a word passed between us.

At last everything was in order, except for Roi and me still sitting there entwined. Then Allen's head appeared in the window, and he said, with a housefatherly grump, "Well, we'll be on our way if these lovebirds can ever let go of each other."

That was at five in the evening. At five in the morning Roi called. "I was just thinking about you," he said, sounding very far away. His sister, visiting, was asleep on the folding cot an inch from the phone. There were other people littered about, and no long phone cords then. I couldn't say much. I wanted to tell him I understood, I would have liked to tell him that I'd always been with him, solid since the beginning, and that the rest was all language—glow, shift, fire or ice, depending—not the root core calm I knew we shared. And that as for me, he'd have to be patient, I was a swollen silence, struggling for words.

But everything stayed inside, with what was growing there, I guess. I told him that I loved him, and good-bye. My mother once said it takes nine months to make a baby and nine months to get over it. At this point I was poised between, wanting only to be delivered so I could start the return trip.

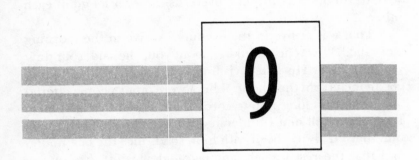

Me mother did finally come to see me, and to meet Roi. She couldn't stay long, she said, eyeing her old kitchen table in the middle of the cluttered room with its folding cot and walls full of thumbtacked announcements. But when Roi arrived she smiled and gave him a warm hello. I was pleased. Later she would say she had "made her peace" with us.

Still it was never an easy peace. I took her to a luncheonette in the neighborhood, where, because I was glad to see her, and wanted to reward her for taking this first step, I confided my natural childbirth plans.

At once she looked down her nose. "You're built just

like I am," she sniffed, "and both my babies had to be *pulled from me.*"

Small, plumpish, wiping the table with a paper napkin, she seemed exactly the same as she'd always been. One of her favorite lines was, "It's nice to be different," but faced with the real thing—me—she inevitably backed down. I felt, as usual, helpless to change her; it was discouraging.

Later I repeated to Roi her comment about natural childbirth, complete with emphasis on "pulled." He dismissed it with a wave of his hand. "She just doesn't understand that you can do anything you *want* to," he grumbled, and I laughed. I'd gone to no classes (there were none that I knew of), done no exercises. But hadn't I always slid by on my will? And what I prized in myself he loved most:

> *My wife is left-handed.*
> *Which implies a fierce de-*
> *termination. A complete other*
> *worldliness. IT'S WEIRD BABY. . . .*
>
> *& now her belly droops over the seat.*
> *They say it's a child. But*
> *I ain't quite so sure.*

The baby was late. I began to doubt it myself. Ten days after the due date, Roi was due in Pennsylvania, to be part of a program at Lehigh University. The Beats were now a campus attraction, worth both money and opportunity. With copies of *Yugen* to sell and my blessing he went.

Joyce, Joel, Max, and the poet Sy Perkoff and his wife, Sara, an artist, were left to mind me. We ate a huge dinner, excited about going to a midnight show of Chaplin's *City Lights*, blacklisted for most of the fifties. I'd never seen it. To seriously consider "masscult"—film, radio, comics, popular music—was a way, we thought, to shape and extend an American aesthetic. Among our downtown friends we counted some filmmakers: Jonas Mekas spent one Sunday morning climbing in and out of our front windows to see if he could film from there (he couldn't).

We never got to *City Lights*, either. About eleven, washing the dishes with Joyce, I was suddenly standing in a puddle, one that had nothing to do with the sink. Shocked, I stared at my drenched shoes. This wasn't *pregnant* anymore, this was *baby*. But after the first panic subsided I felt excited.

Joyce, on the contrary, seemed worried to distraction. As if I'd suddenly aged she guided me gingerly to my new rocking chair (a gift from her). Max, who had a child of his own, and was ever my experienced friend, hovered over me nervously. He kept saying, "Don't worry, you'll do fine," but he was pale as a ghost. Joel took charge. First he phoned Lehigh. The unwilling operator couldn't, she insisted, reach the auditorium. But Oppenheimer could operate too. "Baby," he said, ". . . if I could crawl through the wire. . . ." She promised to try.

Then off we went, to New York Hospital, the six of us like a circus pile in the Perkoffs' little car. I complained all the way about missing the movie. Arrived, still in no pain, I was snatched from my friends and laid out on a gurney, in a corridor. Serious aides, like huge head and footboards, rolled me to the elevator. I couldn't see a thing except the far, dim ceiling and my hump of belly under the sheet. Who was trying to scare me? And why? And there, suddenly, in the empty midnight lobby, were my guardians all in a row, my loyal shepherds of different heights and weights and hairs and sexes and problems and structures—America's terrific new consciousness in arts and letters—and all with the same frightened face! Joel and Max looked grave as rabbis, Joyce had tears in her eyes. Poor darlings! I waved a hand—Cheer up! Cheer up!—and blew them kisses. But they left with never a smile among them!

The "labor nurse" was an Austrian woman, and so-called because her proper midwife title was associated, then, with "backwardness." Yet it all went forward, with her excellent help. She held her hand just above my stomach, saying: "Ze negst breaths vill please kommes to here."

Innovatively, this labor room was also open to my husband, and some hours later in he strode, having received a message, onstage, that his wife had been in an accident. He'd felt all along there'd been a mistake, he told me, still he'd let Ray Bremser—just out of jail—take the turnpike at eighty miles an hour. Poor Roi! He looked exhausted. His new suit was all rumpled. He kept nodding off in his chair beside the bed, but he never let go of my hand until six in the morning, when the midwife, with a gesture worthy of old Vienna, declaimed: "Ah, ze dawn kommes up, und ze baby kommes down!"

Although they shut him out of the main event, Roi—because poets are in the visions business—had already seen his baby two years earlier. He'd written of her "peeking into/ Her own clasped hands," and when the doc-on-duty held her up she seemed perfect proof of how life mimes art, that great believer.

There was general praise for the mom, who'd done it undrugged (like most other women in the world). But *it* was done—and look at this *girl*! An image in the image of the one I love, a "rogue-faced," tearless baby, wide awake and looking! Now she sneezes—she's a *human being*!

We named her Kellie Elisabeth. I couldn't take my eyes off her. I couldn't let go of her. A touch of jaundice two days later burnished her gold, like a temple *putti*. The nurse who brought her in that morning said, "You know why she's this color, don't you?"

Right off the bat I misheard this woman, raising a hostile glare to her kind, concerned face. Then, shamed, I realized she meant the jaundice and I thanked her. But something had changed in me, a quality of response. Suspicion had been a reflex action, a *mis*perception, a paranoia.

"It'll be gone in a day or two," the nurse said. But I knew there'd be a lifetime lesson in it.

That Fourth of July we took the party to Newark and took a picture on the porch steps. In front, leaning on the banister, is a slim, ironic, cheerfully arrogant Roi. I'm standing at the back with the baby, plainly pleased, I've even pulled off my shades for the camera. Seated between the two of us, the Twentieth Street poets, posed with their wives and children, appear to be a large, extended family of which Roi and I are the proud and satisfied parents. In none of our smooth, untroubled faces is there a sign that the life that drew us together could ever shift us around or spin us off. But we knew it.

Just visible in the background of the photo are Anna Lois and Coyt Leroy, the newly titled Gramma and Granddaddy Jones, who had asked, after my wedding, how I'd address them. I wasn't sure what fit. To call them Mr. and Mrs. seemed too formal, first names disrespectful. The day this happened everyone looked at me, waiting for some of my usual mouth. But I went dumb. Roi and his sister Elaine were both grinning. "Well, what do *you* call them?" I asked finally.

"Mama and Daddy." It was the elder Joneses who answered.

There was only one solution I could think of; it seemed presumptuous, of course. "Well, then, uh . . . ," I said, "maybe I'll just, uh . . . could I just, uh . . . call you what everyone else does?"

In that photo of us on the porch, and others taken that Fourth of July, the friendships seem even more intense against suburban sun and shade. Gil in a baseball hero half-crouch, with Joel and Max leaning on him and each other, Elsene and Rena. You can't see the cut-and-run passions, the liaisons, bohemia's slippery, discontinuous social fabric, which was all I had to offer: my mother, visiting the hospital, had burst into tears at the nursery window. Only the Joneses, welcoming me, offered my daughter a history—images, peers, cousins—and whatever else I did or didn't know by that Fourth of July, I knew she was their baby too.

Said Kellie herself, thoughtfully, some years later: "You know, Mommy, your lap is fine. But you ought to sit on *Gramma!*"

To describe maternal love as a "tender affection" was, I decided, only another way to corset passion. The actual feeling was far more volcanic—really, I loved that baby so much it hurt! The cheeks, the brown, shining eyes and the *presence!* I loved to sing to her, to watch her little, still face, listening. Everyone listened:

> *. . . your voice*
> *down the hall, through the window, above*
> *all those trees a light*
> *it seems*
> *& you are singing. What song*
>
> *is that The words*
> *are beautiful.*

The *job* of being Mom—the involvement, time, goo, *stuff*—was astonishing. Like pregnancy and birth, it was rife with professional myth. The day I came home from the hospital, Rena held the baby on her knees. She'd just been fed, and commenced a series of tentative, gummy smiles.

"The nurses said that's gas," I said.

"Gas my ass," scoffed Rena. "It's life that's a gas, right Kellie?" She smiled at the baby, who smiled right back.

One Sunday morning, the tail end of a night before, some of us were strewn around talking, greeting the light as we often did among empty bottles and odd cups sticky with dregs. I must have flaked out, then came to and stuck in the sleep/wake zone, with Chelsea's river-heavy morning air in my nose, daylight pulling at my lids, and in my ears at once a conversation beside me and the baby crying down the hall. "Shouldn't you wake her," a male voice questioned.

I wondered that too. At the party was I also on the job? Would I wake at all? Would I ever fail? Then Rena said, in her quiet, throaty, confident tones: "Oh, she'll wake up herself, she'll hear the baby." And on this wave of reassurance, as if given all the skill I needed, I woke, relieved and certain. There was no magic to it, or mystery—only accommodation. All I had to do was hear the baby.

August 1959. Early one weekday afternoon. Roi is working full time, midtown. I'm alone, staring out the front window. Chelsea, once a farm, then a village separate from Manhattan, is now a neighborhood of brownstone reserve. Above us live two floors of elderly women, quiet as wraiths on the carpeted stairs, and above them *Voice* writer Bill Manville and his girlfriend Rosemarie Santini, whom I hardly ever see. The super and his wife pull our garbage down a dumbwaiter every evening. Yesterday they said: "Jones, Cohen, Kellie, what are you, starting your own UN?"

Once a week I stand in the unemployment line, hoping my breasts won't leak and give me away (nursing mothers are not considered "available"). Most of the time, though, I'm home. Today there's not a soul on the dusty sidewalk, the lines of parked cars stay put, nothing stirs, across the street, in the walled seminary garden. All at once the isolation nearly sends me to my knees. Why had I failed to foresee this? And why, anyway, was I here in the boondocks?

I grabbed the baby and started for Washington Square, where I knew a few mothers to talk to. It was a mile-long walk there, and neither easy nor fast without a foldup stroller or a Snuggli carrier or a backpack. Western women with babies weren't supposed to cover distance. All I had was a big, heavy, hard-to-maneuver carriage, but I got it past the three doors, down the six steps, and all the way to Greenwich and Tenth before the baby woke, hungry and fussing. Although at home I nursed her openly, in the park you had to use the neglected, filthy public toilet. I didn't know whether to turn around or keep going. In a fit of quandariness, I stopped. Kellie, deprived of motion, screamed. My nipples itched and tingled. I would have screamed too, except suddenly, calling my name and waving, Fielding Dawson dashed out of a nearby bar.

I fell into his arms.

"Come watch the ball game," he said. He was with Franz Kline, and they had spotted me through the window.

It was dark and cool inside the unpretentious, empty old place. I hurried to the Ladies' with the baby, leaving the men to wrestle the monster carriage. To get it into the bar proved impossible, however. Returning I found they'd left it outside, and were "watching" it.

Franz was small and fatherly, with a dip of dark hair like my uncles had worn in the forties. He'd fixed Basil and Martha's recalcitrant kerosene heater, cautioned Joyce one night when she went to the Cedar with a badly cut thumb, sent Roi and me to his doctor (T. J. Edlich, Jr., still the artists' practitioner!). I always saw Franz so kindly and calm that I imagined in him a coil, compressed, a wire that sprang to life and moved the paint on his stark, thunderous canvases.

Of all the sons of Black Mountain, Fee had the most stories. "Let me tell you about this one time," he says. He sips his beer and gazes at the ball game a minute, writerly, gathering his thoughts. "So here we are on this dirt road," he says, "in this truck—it was an Army surplus weapons carrier, I believe . . . yes it was. Overhead, a canopy of leaves." He pauses to see if I've got the image; I nod. "So we're on our way home from the store, and Franz is beside me, and we've each got a beer. . . ."

All afternoon, between the slow balls and strikes, with one eye on the carriage outside, I listened.

Before leaving I went back to the Ladies' to nurse the baby again. The pipes to the gravity flush were sweating, the place smelled of ammonia and wet wood, like a latrine. "Hey baby, we're in the outhouse," I whispered, laughing, to Kellie, and she, leaning her head off my breast, laughed too. She'd just learned how.

At which point I burst into tears, a flood I couldn't stop that wet her soft black curls as I rocked us both back and forth, back and forth, trying not to be overheard. Because mothering her I'd neglected the self to whom I'd always been just as kind; I'd put myself in the outhouse. And now I had her with me too, and the way back seemed far and the directions obscure. And nothing in my life was as clear and sweet and simple as Fee, with a beer in his hand, and Franz beside him, in the Army surplus truck, on the dirt road to Black Mountain. . . .

10

In a window of the Figaro Café, in a mess of mikes and lights and cables, Roi and I were positioned one day for an interview with BBC-TV. Once begun, the questioning proceeded without a break; I wasn't asked a word. Inside and out, people collected to watch my husband speak his mind while I sat mute, an embarrassed actress with no lines. This had never happened before. Was it the baby on my lap? Were mothers automatically overlooked? Or just looked *at*— was it "See the interracial freaks"? But I kept smiling. I didn't want to spoil Roi's scene.

Roi had a number of scenes. He had a job writing technical manuals, the kind of situation known as a "slave." He went every day and brought home his pay. He brought a young woman from his office once; they arrived laughing and sharing a mandarin orange.

His interests kept him moving. If he came home after work, he'd invariably go out again. He and Frank O'Hara had become good friends. They were equal and alike: small, spare, original, confident, stuck on themselves for good reasons. With urbane witty Frank, Roi was free of the slough of domesticity, the broody inelegance of playpen clutter, my milky left shoulder. One evening as the two of them were leaving I threw my arms around him, and out of my mouth sprang "Don't be late." Beside me Frank stiffened. But I already knew what I'd done. "How's that for a line," I said. Frank looked amazed. "I thought you were *serious*," he said.

When Roi learned I'd given my *Partisan* job to Joyce, he said, "Why didn't you ask *me*?" The question surprised me. Then I felt guilty that I hadn't thought of it. "Why didn't you make the suggestion?" I said. "I never thought you'd want to do it—I mean all that clerical work . . ."

"I can do anything you can do," he snapped. "You'd be nothing without me." He rushed from the room.

So I wasn't surprised to learn that he and Diane Di Prima were lovers—but the first affair cuts the cake, nothing else is ever as sharp. And Diane was everything I wasn't. To begin she was single, and single women know, as the blues say, when to raise their window high. I liked her because she was smart and quick to laugh, and enjoyed her bisexual life (although she tended to wear lovers like chevrons). Unmarried, she was raising a daughter. Unusual, her family hadn't turned on her; she took me to Brooklyn once to meet her grandmother. I never knew how she lived, working only occasional odd jobs. But Diane's life was her lit.

At first I thought it had to be all my fault. Because the two of them loved Ezra Pound and as a Jew I just *couldn't*. Because I broke my jade ring in the shower. You were supposed to hold your man and I hadn't. It took me a while to gather my wits, to think about *me*. Me! Me! Me! What must I do?

I didn't demand that he end the affair or leave. Among my friends I counted as many affairs as marriages, everyone was hot and mixed up. One night at the Cedar, with narcoleptic Roi asleep on her shoulder, Diane said, in a burst of generosity: "Hettie's a great lady, because she doesn't bug her man."

But I thought about Billie's blues, about love like a faucet. Why had I forgotten? What had suckered me into illusion?

"An evil word," Roi wrote of love, and he was right. "Turn it backwards / see, see what I mean?" The trouble was he always wrote the truth.

Max went to live with Joel and Rena, and Fee got a loft, and we got a new boarder, that fall of 1959, a college friend of Roi's named A.B. Spellman, who wouldn't be known by anything but his initials, the second accented. A.B. was tall, solid, and friendly, he'd chosen poetry in New York over law school in the South, and he could overwhelm an argument with his basso profundo voice: "Hey hey *hey, wait* a minute, just *wait* a minute . . ." Joel managed to sleep on Roi's desk, A.B. survived the bathtub. As a writer he was Roi's challenge and sidekick, and he quickened the mix of the Black Bourgeoisie with Black Mountain College. When saxophonist Sonny Rollins's record "Way Out West" came out—with Sonny on the jacket in a ten-gallon hat and chaps— A.B. sprang to his feet waving the cover around. "An image that must be *seen!*" he roared. "Put the lost black cowboys on the silver screen! Move over John Wayne! Go Tonto!"

To his great credit, A.B. Spellman didn't resist his soft side. He liked good women. He introduced us to Sara Golden, who married the poet Paul Blackburn and later published as Sara Blackburn. To me, A.B. was an easy, even-tempered friend, and Kellie, after Da*Da* and Ma*Ma*, called him Ba*By*. When my unemployment ran out, and *Partisan* offered me part-time work, he volunteered to mind the house. I accepted at once—although I'd never heard of any woman trusting her child to a man while she went to a job.

I left home wearing nun's oxfords, a dress of upholstery brocade, and large, round, black-rimmed spectacles. A kid late for school, running past me, called over his shoulder, "Hey lady, your glasses are on upside down!"

Two other women were now crowded with me into the cluttered rooms on Union Square, our salaries covered by the Congress for Cultural Freedom, later revealed as a CIA front to shore up the anticommunist New York intellectuals. Among the younger editors and contributors to *Partisan* were some who also appeared in *Yugen*. "Send me some of those West Coast books you mentioned during that steamy happy half hour I spent in your office," wrote Kenneth Koch from Greece.

William Phillips later regretted not publishing more of the Beats, but neither he nor Philip Rahv would consider any of the work I urged on Kenneth, nor would most of the younger editors, the rising neoconservatives, who simply assumed that they were American lit and I wasn't. "The male whale," said one grave academic, "is the only mammal equipped with a bone in his penis."

Some of the downtown—male—artists played softball. Roi played center field. "He was our leader," writes third baseman Fielding Dawson. "He wore short pants, and showed his knobby knees, and allowed himself to be amused by his image of himself as Willie Mays." A typical lineup would have included Joel Oppenheimer, pitching; on first base painter Jim Johnson (Joyce Glassman's boyfriend-to-be-husband); painter Emilio Cruz, shortstop; sculptor John Chamberlain catching; also Gilbert Sorrentino, Paul Blackburn, and Joe Early (who was editing the magazine *Noose*). There were others, of course, scattered about the huge, fenced-in field on Houston and West Broadway, flexing their muscles, sweating, squinting seriously into the bright afternoon in their dirty T-shirts. Discounting beards and hangovers, you could have put them on the cover of the *Saturday Evening Post*.

Wives and women artists and friends sat on the sidelines at the ball games, never again to play with men, expected to lose the bodies we'd used as children, expected, eventually, to grow up and get into our girdles. Fortunately dance, being art, was permitted artists' wives. Rena and I studied with Donya Feuer, who was then the partner of Paul Sanasardo (and later, in Europe, a leading neoexpressionist).

If at school I'd learned to breathe it was Donya who taught me to stand. One night she asked us each to cross the floor alone, an imagined jug of water on our heads and our feet in sand. The weight of the world's water in that jar, and my feet in my shifting life, I crossed. "Now who was the best?" Donya asked—and everyone called my name and applauded!

But why—I thought afterward—why only in a roomful of women had I succeeded? The long mirror reflected the class in their black tights, conscientious, lively Donya at the head, Rena beside me. "Star of the show!" she teased. But I knew I was looking to score elsewhere. I just laughed and decided I'd have to try harder.

At the Cedar you ran the gauntlet past the bar to the booths at the back, or, on a busy night, pushed through a solid wall of people. Rena and I always went there after class. Sometimes the place was filled to capacity, and you had to wait on the street to get in, or get word to the owners (who were proud of their regulars and obliging). Apart from being Mecca to movers and shakers, there was nothing distinguished about the Cedar with its framed prints of early American scenes on the walls; it would have been a dark, nondescript bar like a hundred others except for the stories about Jackson Pollock destroying the door to the men's room. Myself I loved the mess of it, the murk of smoke and emotion, the quick, laughing flirtations, flattery from men I admired. One night Willem DeKooning gave me a rose he'd been holding. Surprised, I twirled it in my hands a moment. What did one do? I stuck it in my hatband. He liked that.

Among the shoulder-to-shoulder boozers sex was easy to come by. First I tried it straight. I sat down next to a curly-haired painter I liked. We said hello. After that he said, "I'd like to take you home." I said, "Sure." He choked on his shot, then downed it, said, "Phew," and we left and hit the sack. It was terrific. "You won't tell your husband?" he said, hailing me a cab home later.

To find comfort in all that fervor and self-love wasn't easy, but that's what I wanted. Mike Kanemitsu was a small, slender man, like a reed flute, like the tones of his Japanese name, Matsumi. He was older than I, a close friend of Frank O'Hara, and also of Kerouac. He'd given Roi a painting for the cover of *Projective Verse*, an essay of Olson's Totem was publishing. The evening he offered to let us keep the original, he and I were seated on either side of Roi at the bar. "For you and your *wife*," Mike emphasized, bending around to make sure I heard. "Yeah, yeah," said Roi, laughing.

One night I left the Cedar with Mike and went to his loft, not far from where I lived in Chelsea. On the living side he'd built a self-contained room, a box one entered up a couple of steps. Inside, in warm silence, soft beds surrounded a carpeted well. Mike had been married once, his wife had died. I didn't know what I could be for him, but he didn't seem to mind. "But don't you want to be *happy*?" I protested.

He leaned over me, his dark eyes amused. "Happy?" he said. "What makes you think that's the answer?"

Lover or wife my skills didn't change, though. I'd sometimes visit Mike in the afternoon, on my way home from work. One day he'd just finished a painting, and hauled me into his studio with the same excitement I knew at home. "Look! It's done!" "Beautiful!" I said, because it was—all ochres and textures, and had about it, abstract or no, the feel of a fine animal. I told Mike this. "You're right!" he shouted. "I'm calling it 'Coyote'! How come you *understand* so much!"

But Roi began to resent my dance class. First he said I got too dressed up, then he showed up late so I missed it. One evening after he went out, I left A.B. in charge and went to Mike's. At 3 A.M. Roi came pounding at Mike's door, enraged, *offended*, his face all contorted, his neat self all disarranged. He grabbed my jacket, threw it on my shoulders, and started to push me out.

"Let's be civilized about this, Roi," said Mike. "Have a drink."

"Cut the bullshit, motherfucker, I'm not a civilized man!" Roi yelled.

I left with him—it seemed the only sensible thing to do. All through Chelsea's long, deserted blocks he screamed at me: "Whore! Bitch! Dumb! Woman!" I shouted back, of course—mostly about Diane—but he wouldn't respond to that, and just as we reached our door he proclaimed, at the top of his lungs, that he'd never slept with her.

A.B. streaked past us, pulling on his pants. I reeled into the bedroom, flung off my clothes, and lay down. Roi was smashing plates and overturning chairs. I heard something splinter. The baby—how had she managed to sleep through all this?

At last it occurred to me that what he really wanted to do was hit *me*, and I called this out to him. He came down the hall and stood in the doorway, affecting his sophisticated, slim lounge, as if he hadn't just aced all the coffee cups. "Look at you in your black underpants!" he burst out and that riled him up again. "Going out like a whore in sexy underwear!" he yelled.

A great hilarity rose in me—I almost laughed out loud. *He* was the middle-class one—everything he liked to blame on me! "Shut up you'll wake the baby," I said, and went to confront him. We stood in the hallway glaring at each other. It was just getting light. "Go ahead, hit me, go ahead," I dared, not thinking he would. But to my surprise (and his own) he did, and his slap forced my head against the wall, *thunk*, and then—as he wrote in the story "Going Down Slow"—he grabbed me and we "stood holding each other for about thirty minutes."

Look at us there, if you will, in that chilly spring dawn. Two twenty-five-year-old kids with a kid, in the middle of a lot of commotion. Do you see race in this? Have you forgotten? It would get worse. We must have known, the way we hung on to each other.

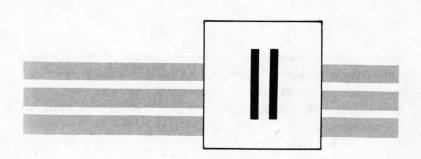

"You'll be the one family in ten to complete the long form," said the bald man—a census taker, heralding the sixties, peering cautiously into the room. At the table, glasses half off his nose, pale bearded Joel was folded into a chair with a book; beyond, in the front room, Roi was in his socks reading the *Times*, and A.B., in shirttails and wrinkled khakis, was napping on the couch. Each was easily a man at home. The census man slid me a nervous smile. At 8 P.M. on a Tuesday, what kind of "family" was this? Suddenly Kellie, as if determined to be counted, began to scoot toward him in her walker. The man jumped back, thrust a fistful of forms at me, and fled!

And we all gathered round—found. "Indicate whether

anyone in your family is of mixed origin," was one instruction, with the example "part-Hawaiian." "Part-*Hawaiian!*" Roi shouted. "What the fuck is *that?*"

We decided—after some debate—to enter "part-white" for Kellie and let the paperkeepers guess the remainder. Though in real life, as I'd been ready for (I thought), the one-half had indeed made her whole. At birth, on her hospital record, she was listed as "Negro female."

Philip Rahv had a theory that a woman who wants a baby would discover, if she questioned herself, that what she really wants is a cat. Surprising in a literary man, among other joys this overlooks the rediscovery of language. For me, talking to Kellie perfectly balanced William and Philip's high-culture biases. "*B*aby," she said importantly, pointing to one in a carriage, and then, with a grin at her favorite uncle, "Ba*by!*"

Most Saturdays Kellie and I went to Newark, on the Hudson Tubes (now the PATH train). I'd explain the tunnel under the river and name the world as we crossed the meadows, with her beside me nose to the pane, absorbed—and lovely, I thought, in her hand-me-down red overalls. With her round face and dark eyes and open, direct, equable gaze, she looked like Roi (and even more like his mother), and maybe it was because she didn't resemble me that I marveled at how *like* me she was, how female and how conscious in that little body. The way I'd been in mine and never told. I wanted to give her every word.

There on the train, pair by pair, the eyes of the world drifted in and settled on us. Nothing can ready you for this. With Roi I had the thing licked, but with Kellie it was different; she was both threat and potential victim, and I had to protect her. It felt, sitting there, as if we were wearing a skin of public opinion, that stuck and clung and pressed and forced a change in the way you could breathe—think of the words *strong attraction*. As Greer and Cobbs would explain in *Black Rage* (1968), this evokes a physical defense, a necessary response, a "normal" paranoia. One Saturday, not long after the census, a man across from us on the train wore a hard, angry look; he knew what we were but he didn't want to think it. I thought right away of "part-Hawaiian"; it was clear that the one-half mattered to this man, that by blurring the we/they line we'd swollen the ranks of those he'd have to define. I couldn't stand his eyes—not on me but on her—*her*, my apple-cheeked, brown-limbed, loving, talkative child. My girl! I wanted to kill him! *Kill him!!*

I got to Newark exhausted. Gramma laughed and patted my head and made coffee. "You'll get used to it," she said. I didn't believe her.

A couple of years later, waiting in New York one early morning for that same train, we drew the attention of a woman wearing a garish crust of pancake makeup. She circled us first, then stood and stared. I ignored her. I was, indeed, used to it. But then she spoke: "Are ya Puerto Rican, dearie?"

"No," I said calmly.

By then, Kellie had seen hundreds of those curious eyes, and already had a supersense for the tones of certain words. The woman with all the makeup on finally—and triumphantly—made up her mind. "I know—you're *colored*," she said.

Said Kellie: "Hah hah, you're colored *orange*."

Gramma supervised, for the Newark Housing Authority, that cutting edge called "tenant relations." She knew a lot of people all over town. Saturday afternoons she'd drive us around, showing me what she thought I should see while she showed off her baby. From the hilly suburban Newark I'd known as a child we went to bleak, neglected urban projects, where the public spaces bristled with clotheslines rather than benches or monkey bars, as if laundry—on the tenement model—were the single most regarded communal activity. Newark surprised me with unexpectedly rural sections, rows of tiny rough frame homes that looked like the South—the streets, ignored in the affluent fifties, that Michael Harrington would present in 1962 as *The Other America.*

Gramma—Anna Lois—was called by her middle name. The Lois Jones I came to know was a woman of strong opinions who was also one of the best of teachers; she never preached, she just kept steadily driving: to club meetings, clinics, church basements, bars, picnics in cement courtyards with lots of kids and chicken. Working mothers, most. Right away they let me know that assuming their burden was foolish: "Why *this*?" they said, pinching Kellie. "Wasn't being Jewish bad enough?" But then they would wink and haul me into the kitchen. I had to rest my feet, hand over that *baby*, and have a little potato salad, honey. They fed me kind acceptance at first, then praise and love and laughs and I stuffed myself full.

Roi seldom joined these visits; for him, Newark was the past with which he presently grappled. But I felt I understood him better: in New York he was often the only black person in a room, in Newark, for me, the picture reversed.

I learned a lot Saturdays—as much or more than I did at my weekday job. In Newark I read *Ebony* and *Jet*, and saw what had happened with Africa denied, with light skin and straight hair given pride of place, and I saw, as Roi had warned, how that could drive you crazy if you bought it. "O, / generation of fictitious / Ofays," he'd written. "Beware the evil sun / . . . turn you black." But racist thought was in all things, even in language; racism was, as it would come to be described, institutionalized, and it seemed that now I could see it everywhere. The most "enlightened" were complicit. This story was told of two New Critics: one said he had to be going, couldn't keep his mother's chauffeur waiting. "Chauffeur?" sniffed the other. "That's not a chauffeur . . . that's just an ordinary field negra."

△ △ △

In 1955, in Montgomery, Alabama, a few weeks after I'd finished college and come north, a seamstress named Rosa Parks refused to move to the back of the bus that was taking her home. Her action triggered a boycott, already planned, that went on for thirteen months and was resoundingly successful. "My feet may be tired," said one old lady, "but my soul is resting." But Montgomery's buses didn't run anywhere near the Morton Street I reached shortly after that boycott ended, and though from then on the South had continued its rumble, we were more involved in our own.

In 1960, someone leaving the city gave us a small TV— our first. We'd been raised on radio: "Saturday mornings we listened to . . . *Let's Pretend*," Roi wrote, "& I, the poet, still do, Thank God!" We still listened to "Matt Dillon" every Sunday night. TV, at least at first, looked a lot like the truth. As children of the forties we'd missed organized labor's bloody beginnings, the Depression's deprivations. But by 1960 the student-led lunch-counter sit-ins had begun. Once again violence was a daily feature in peaceful America, and TV, that useful tool, could make it happen in front of your face. Day after day the students leaned on Formica counters in Nashville. They were young, younger than we, led by a woman of twenty-two. Groups of jeering whites spilled sugar in their hair, and smeared ketchup and mustard on their neatly pressed, properly fifties conservative clothes.

The rest of us watched. Roi and I were home alone one Sunday afternoon, our eyes on a stern, dark, dignified boy, and a girl whose dress was dripping something viscous. They seemed like such kids to me; the girl swallowed hard, you could tell she was scared. Behind them a crowd nearly out of control mugged for the camera and tried to shout each other down. Just then Granddaddy came to the door with Kellie, who'd spent the night in Newark. She ran to me and I grabbed her up and held her. I'd never imagined such risks, I'd seen her from my own perspective not from this. The boy, shoved from behind, bent his head to the counter.

I glanced at Roi who was glued to the set, jaw clenched, the way he always looked when he was angry.

Around this growing concern, the pot that was bohemia boiled. I watched the women and knew them best. Rena holed me up in the study one night. "There's something I have to tell you," she said, avoiding my eye. "I'm not going to live with Joel anymore, I'm going to live with Max and we're splitting for New Mexico."

I was stunned. I'd known nothing of this. All I could say was "Oh, wow." We stood in front of the bookshelves, separated by our domestic dilemmas, mute among all those words.

"So," Rena said finally, in a low, strained voice. Her face was still averted, her easy body rigid. "So," she repeated, "I'd like to give you my dresser."

They left soon, the dresser remained for years. How I missed Rena, and Max too. Lonely Joel stood in my bedroom doorway one night. "Just let me lie down with you and hold you," he said. "I won't do anything."

While in jail Ray Bremser had learned to write, and was paroled when Roi agreed to "give him a job on *Yugen*." Ray's wife was named Bonnie. They arrived one Friday to spend the night, a tall, gaunt, long-faced hipster with his pretty, snub-nosed, brunette chick. Bonnie was so in love that sometimes passion overwhelmed her; she'd close her eyes to contain it, press her head against his sleeve. Of all the women I knew she seemed the most downwardly mobile, looking less to find new than lose old, shed some self she could no longer stand. "Do you shudder after you pee?" she and Ray asked me once, dissolving in laughter. "Sometimes we pee together!" But Bonnie wanted, even in bohemia, everything a woman could do. She bore a baby too small at birth to take home, then kept up her milk for a month with a pump—and the first time she nursed at a party, her well-primed breasts squirted clear across the room. But soon she fled with the baby and Ray to Mexico, on a false rumor involving his parole. I never knew that subsequent Bonnie, the bleached, broke, skin-and-bones Bonnie about whom she wrote in her memoir, *Troia* (Mexican slang for adventuress or whore). But in this story of a mother's life on the road the romance goes and the baby is left at the border. Bonnie herself made it back. That arc of her milk stayed on my mind.

Rochelle Owens was having a hard time. Fielding Dawson, sprawled in a low chair, was yanking at the hem of her skirt. "C'mere, lessee what you're made of," he said. Tall, attractive, determined, Rochelle was new to the house; her work would be included soon in Totem's *Four Young Lady Poets*. Yet there was a frailty to her, she seemed not only embarrassed but bewildered and reluctant to be rude. She swatted at Fee a few times but he kept his grip, and then her face got red and I thought she'd cry in a minute. "Let her alone, that's *her* business!" I yelled.

Roi has written of my "scolding" the men. But I also liked to give up my position. One lovely spring weekend we left the baby in Newark and went to Bennington for a reading. How did I come to be on David Smith's lap, as monumental as his sculpture, in a kitchen where all the women were making salad while all the rest of the men made a beer run? And why did I have no shame, cuddling there, was I Daddy's little girl, cutting celery? "Put the tops in too," he said. "But they're bitter." "They won't be, in the dressing." They never are.

It was later that night, after the reading and the party and the numberless beers, that the nightmare real world crept in.

Roi and I had gone to bed in a room we'd been told was free. As usual after too much booze, in the middle of the night I was suddenly sick and not finding a toilet hit a sink. Unexpectedly, at dawn, a man came in. I drifted awake to his mutter about the mess. Roi and I were under a sheet, only up to our waists. I felt too sick to move. The man came over to the bed. Guiltily I pretended sleep but I think he knew I could hear. "Look at her, naked in the arms of her Negro," he said, and I couldn't tell whether he was drunk or mad, so I kept my eyes shut and he left, and I never mentioned him, not wanting to be thought a coward, or a fool. It was April 1960 then. In the following year, eleven African countries would declare their independence, altering the world's political balance, and the civil rights movement in America would reflect this change. Sometimes I think of that man at Bennington, out there with this picture of us in his head. Is he guilty now? Does he still hate us? I always saw him as a sixties harbinger, like the census man.

The year before, Totem had published *JAN 1st 1959: FIDEL CASTRO*, a pamphlet meant as a tribute. The title was Roi's idea. Fee did the cover and I set the thing up for offset; there were poems by Kerouac, Loewinsohn, Oppenheimer, Sorrentino, and Roi himself, and prophecy from Max Finstein:

> *Los barbudos!*
> *The pretty girls*
> *will belong*
> *to you*

Word of this publication reached Cuba's cultural arm, the Casa de las Americas. In the summer of 1960, Roi was invited by the new Cuban government to travel there with a group of Negro-American artists (including the painter Edward Clark, with whom we became friends). "Greetings from Revolutionary Cuba!" sang out the confirming postcard, and the trip, for Roi, proved effective as any draft notice. In his words, years later, a turning point in his life. But then we all still believed in the power of the word, and he that one could choose one's weapon. For the moment, going to Cuba just sharpened his pen. One of his poems was printed in *Lunes de Revolución*, the Havana newspaper; he did indeed meet Fidel; and he even—like *white* folks—got an actual sunburn that peeled. He phoned me with great excitement, on fire to explain over the staticky wire what we were missing in our America, and how he envied the Latin Americans' easy nationalism. All this went into an essay when he returned, titled "Cuba Libre," which was published in *Evergreen Review*, later won the Longview Award for journalism, and really gave him a leg up, since apart from that letter in *Partisan*, and a poem in an earlier *Evergreen*, all his work had appeared thus far in *Yugen* and a few other little magazines. "Cuba Libre" was his first lengthy piece of prose, and like everyone else I found it insightful; it seemed so clear, and the Roi I loved was so sincerely *in* it.

And I thought he'd taken a lot on his slender back. He wrote of being on a long, hot train ride up to the Sierra Maestra, and while all the other passengers were calling back and forth their national pride—"Viva Mexico!" "Viva Brazil!" "Viva Argentina Libre"—he sat wondering what he might say of America, and himself, and finally yelled, "Viva Calle Cuarenta y dos!" "Viva Cinco Punto!" And along with his layer of skin he lost some illusions. On the train the Latin Americans nearly had him in tears, he said, jeering at his explanations of how he made art to cultivate his soul. One of them screamed that the hungry people of his country would move him enough to write poems. Roi knew those

Newark streets far better than I, and I knew how he might have felt, hearing that.

One early morning later that summer I wheeled the kid in her stroller to the bank we used at Tenth and Twenty-third. That part of Chelsea was out of the way then, streets of warehouses, rooms for sailors between ships. The bank seldom had more than a few customers at once. I entered in a hurry, headed for one of the managers with a seven-dollar out-of-state check to cash. Very official, the check, from a library, and it was going to buy me a pair of sandals to replace the ones I was wearing mended with tape, which I hoped would last until I could get back home and then across town to work. Roi had left his job for the Cuba trip, and was now on unemployment, happily writing, which made us both feel better but meant money was even scarcer.

Someone had beat me to the manager, a man who turned as I crossed the carpeted margin, and I saw it was Jimmy Baldwin, who also lived in Chelsea then and who was probably broke too at that time, even though his work had been so well received. He looked drawn, almost ill, his heavy eyes sad and dark-circled, but when he bent to the baby his face lit, as if here, in this new life, were reason enough. And it was then that I saw, over Jimmy's back and the tight cap of his hair, the half-dozen idle, gawking tellers at the end of the room. I was reeling that morning, from the humid August air, from my strong yet conflicting feelings about all the affairs, the harsh, constant assault of *opinion*, the whirl of drink and drugs and parties (we'd even been written up by Kerouac in an article for *Holiday* magazine). All of it stopped dead for that moment, as Jimmy reached to Kellie, and the tellers in the cages and the manager behind his desk withdrew and withdrew and withdrew, and I stood uneasily among them, alone and barefoot on that deep, unfamiliar carpet.

We decided to move that fall when the lease was up. I wanted to live on the Lower East Side, among all our friends; I was tired of Chelsea's high rent and packaged salami, and yearned for the Second Avenue Deli, and fresh bread, and the Five Spot and the Fourth Avenue bookshops. Although Roi agreed, something kept him reluctant; maybe he didn't want me too close to the scene. "Oh, you just want to live near Joyce," he snapped one day when we were discussing it, and I laughed—why deny me my girlfriend? Then he got flustered and turned away to hide it, and that was how we decided. Since he wasn't working he went looking; I trusted him to find something good and he did.

Like the typewriter on Morton Street, I left something behind with this move too. Our new phone was the first to be listed under Roi's name. Two years before, Hettie Cohen had simply moved her account, but now that she owed a sizable sum to Ma Bell for those indistinct calls from Havana, it was convenient—no, necessary—to ditch her. I didn't think I'd mind; after two years I was used to being Jones, and was listed that way on the *Partisan* masthead. But when the bill collector called my office, looking for in-debt Miss Cohen, I had to be the one to tell him. "No, she's no longer with us," I said coolly. "Yes, she did work here, but I don't know where she is now." For a moment—the words out and gone—I felt a terrible loss, as if I'd dismissed an old friend. But it was done; that was it for Hettie Cohen. I hung up and called home, and Roi made a big, comforting joke about her departure.

Still the incident nagged me. Poor discarded Hettie Cohen. With all her grand ambition, all she'd ever "become" was Hettie Jones. I felt I owed her. The Friday before we moved I went out at lunchtime with my take-home thirty-seven dollars, determined to buy a desk, my first. Down on Avenue B, in a huge dark store full of used furniture, I found one the right height, oak with a carved front and a number of useful-looking compartments.

The big, beefy man who ran the shop was looking at me with that special face reserved for women who didn't know their place, their proper length of heel, hair, hem. "How much for the desk?" I asked.

"It's not a desk, it's a secretary," he said.

I wanted nothing to do with that word. "How much is the desk?" I said again, as if he hadn't spoken.

"Four dollars," he said, shrugging.

I handed him the milk money, feeling proudly tender toward myself, and more like writing than I had in a long while. Donald Allen's *The New American Poetry* anthology had just been published, and I was spending time over it, pleased by the familiar names and the poems that had appeared first in *Yugen*. My own name was in it too, in the titles of two poems Roi had written about me. So far I couldn't write about him, but to stop *trying*—what a shame on Hettie Cohen. When I got back to the office I glanced through the book again and then typed out Olson's opening words:

What does not change / is the will to change

FOURTEENTH STREET

12

Manhattan has many real and imagined boundaries, but Fourteenth Street in 1960 seemed one of the clearest: a straight road the width of the island, east to west between uptown and down. We boasted of seldom needing to cross it. Money had built its eastern blocks a hundred years before, and so a legacy of elegance remained, more or less still inhabited but faded and crumbling slowly among hard-pressed retail stores and upstairs pool halls. On a Sunday in October 1960, Granddaddy rented a truck and moved us into one of these old brick buildings, between First and Second avenues, almost the last with its original brownstone stoop, on the south side of the street looking north. Earlier twentieth-century artists—Reginald Marsh, Max Weber, Raphael Soyer—had lived in attics along Fourteenth Street; ours was a parlor floor, above a vacant store with dusty, discarded shoeboxes in the window. When we arrived I sat on the worn stoop minding the goods while the truck was unloaded. Down the block I could see Stuyvesant Town, an island of middle-class, segregated housing, and, in the sky across the street, beyond Con Edison's clock tower, the Empire State and Chrysler buildings. I felt suddenly jolted awake, as if stationed at the front, with all of downtown at my back, and as soon as we were safely in I flung aside the shutters on the tall casement windows that faced the street. It seemed wise to keep an eye out.

I was still looking several days later when a flash of new color caught me, a morning I was late for work and running. Overnight the wide, dim window of the vacant store had been transformed. A proscenium curtain was painted on it—in royal blue, with white crescent moons and stars—and in a semicircle stage center, artfully lettered, PROFESORA LUZ, PALMISTA, READER & ADVISER. On the ledge underneath was the color I'd seen, a swath of red velvet strewn with flowers and figurines, and behind all this, hunched in a chair, sat the Profesora herself—strong-featured, kerchiefed, lost in thought. Then noticing me she was suddenly all smiles, a playful middle-aged woman, beckoning. But I just smiled and waved and rushed on. The soft Romany of this woman's family, their laughter and argument and incredible music came up through the floor all the time we were there. But I never would let them look in my eyes. My future was *mine*.

Anyway there was plenty of present, and to regard it an enormous, ornate, gilt-edged mirror, four feet wide and floor-to-ceiling, bolted to the wall between the two front windows. The house itself was long, wide, and open like a loft, and the mirror gave the whole thing back. You were always coming upon yourself. Kellie would climb on her trike and drive hell-bent toward it: twenty pounds of consciousness, grinning like crazy, hurtling through a million cubic feet. I called Fourteenth Street the Court: hard to live in but great for games.

It was also cold in all those (unheated) cubic feet, and sometimes the Profesora or one of her daughters would knock at our door, and heroic Roi would run downstairs with his butane torch to thaw the pipes before they froze solid and burst. The grateful gypsies would always offer him coffee and a free reading, but like me he'd decline—I think he also knew some stories he didn't want told. The plumbing froze because it was an afterthought in that house: our bathroom was crammed in a piece of the hallway under the stairs, and as you sat on the toilet, enthroned above an eight-inch slab of cement, the neighbors went up and down right over your head. It was the kitchen of 324 East Fourteenth that I liked, an addition at the back with a gas heater stuck in a high, wide hearth, where the bricks held heat as they were meant to. All day the room was flooded with light, from two enormous windows that overlooked a forest of weeds and a long, tangled stand of ailanthus—poverty trees Roi called them.

Aptly. We never had more than a dollar, it was hard to manage the fifty for the rent, and someone still owes Granddaddy for that truck. For a while, until we got a water heater, to bathe I sat in the deep side of the double kitchen sink with my feet in the shallow side, in water poured from pails on the stove.

I put my new desk in the corner of the room intended for dining, adjacent to the baby's room, Roi's study, the kitchen, and the phone. For each I had a set of limbs and senses, some of which were to work simultaneously. As the painter Paula Modersohn-Becker notes in her journal: "I am writing this . . . in my kitchen, cooking a roast of veal."

Tense, low-voiced, frowning, facing each other a foot apart, up to our ears in mutual, prideful life, we're standing, Roi and I, with the threshold of the kitchen doorway between us. It's the end of October 1960. *Partisan*, tired of my erratic arrangements, has asked me to work full time—or not at all.

Roi's head is down, he's fooling with a pencil in his hands.

"What do you think?" I say.

"You don't have to do it," he says.

But we both know it's either me or him.

Every contour he becomes is so familiar to me, every attitude he takes I can read as though it were words. He's thinking of himself, of course, of having to give up this progress he's made, he's now the only working Negro jazz critic, he writes record reviews, liner notes, articles, his opinions are already solicited, he's hot and getting hotter, there is, probably, no one quite like him in the world. Lincoln Kirstein, maker of many careers, has just written thanking him for his participation in a program at City Center and hoping they might become friends. Roi has everything except money and even a little of that may be on its way: he's slated soon for the basic incentive given to young black artists, the Whitney Opportunity Fellowship.

If I were he, I wouldn't want to give up any of this. And neither do I want him to, I'm as proud of him as he is. "It's stupid for you to get a job now," I say.

But then, all at once in his reluctant shrug of assent, there's that other side to him, the one of which I'm suspicious, the one that wants to take care of it all himself, to have his woman by the fire—and his other women where he finds them, it's all part of the set. And women adore this young, so excitingly *black*, up-and-coming event. Especially those who'd like to taste forbidden fruit with such a *nice* guy. Part of his charm is the way he treats them: he's kind, polite, good-humored, gentle. So they just can't help it and neither can he and they're all over him like ants in the honey.

There's no vocabulary for me that I know of, standing there in the doorway. A little of Billie's blues maybe, but mostly I'm still dealing with instinct, flashes of inspiration and dread. I can't tell him why. I just shake my head.

"No," I say. "No, I'd rather work."

He scowls, he doesn't say a word. This is the best decision, of course, but no doubt he also feels guilty, thinking he's sending me out to pay the rent.

"Really it'll be okay," I offer. "Really." And with this reassurance for him I understand, at last, that for me everything is different than for him, even dependency a different risk. To one of us a job is a slave, to the other it's a guarantee of freedom. And it's his male pride, with all that this entails, against my freedom to take it or leave it. He has lots of ways to make his side up, but I can only lose once. And I won't.

This was a Thursday. I resurrected the previous Sunday's classifieds; there were three numbers listed under "Child Care Situations Wanted." For a moment I listened to Roi scat-singing and stamping his feet and typing in his window-less room. Risky, I thought, both to find a stranger and to let one into our life. But I picked up the phone. Of the three, one person was still available. *Why*, I thought anxiously.

Next day I greeted a tall, stout, placid-faced, thirtyish woman, stolid and country, from an island off the coast of Jamaica and now living in Queens. She was accompanied by an older aunt who appeared to be her sponsor, but unlike her aunt she hadn't a hint of sophistication about her, in clothes or manner. She didn't have much to say. But she wanted the job very much, said her eyes when she saw Kellie, and I could see what it meant to her, to care for a child who might have been hers. And so we agreed. We split my salary down the middle. With her own ideas of position, she kept us formal all the while we knew her: she was always Miss Bailey, and we were Mr. and Mrs. Jones.

Several years later Paul Krassner drew a comic of us for *The Realist*, his magazine of social satire. The strip showed Roi as SuperSpade, me as Lady, and Miss Bailey as Aunt Jemima. But we were all just doing what we had to. I think Miss Bailey enjoyed the action at our house; we probably beat a steady diet of Queens. She was friendly and curious, and soon came out from behind her passivity, and taught me to cook pot roast and how to use hot sauce, and regaled us with tales of her home, where cashews grew wild for the picking, not salty in grease-stained bags like those I'd bring from the nut store on sleazy Fourteenth Street, the divider. Miss Bailey herself didn't cotton to divisions. On her own steam, she took Kellie to a playground in Stuyvesant Town, where she'd heard there were activities for toddlers. But even though all the other nannies were also black, after a week Miss Bailey was asked to take her kid and leave.

When I got home that day she was furious. "How can they just throw us out?" she demanded.

"Because they know we can't possibly live there," I said.

She shrugged this off. "They only did it," she said, "because Kellie kept winning the games."

Go 'head, Auntie. Persevere, Miss Clotelle Bailey.

I n November that year my mother came to visit. We'd seen her twice since Kellie's birth, but this was the first time she'd brought someone else: her sister Lee Steinberg from Newark, with whom I'd spent time as a child. They'd kindly arrived with my childhood mementos—everything I'd intentionally left—a trunkful rescued from the attic of the house in Laurelton prior to its sale.

Friendly enough, these mothers of mine, and pleasant to Kellie. But after dragging in the trunk and some boxes, they seemed at a loss. My mother was fifty-eight then, my aunt a few years older. They'd been raised near the Brooklyn waterfront, their divorced mother sometimes took in boarders; they'd seen sights they had neatly forgotten. At my kitchen table, on its very last legs and improbably small in the formal dimensions of that house, the two of them sat drinking tea from jelly glasses and trying not to seem uncomfortable, looking in vain for something familiar, like chandeliers or curtains. I had nothing for them to admire or dispute, and knew I never would, but I myself was wishing for—not their approval, which I had never wanted and therefore didn't expect—but some satisfaction for them, a hint that would comfort them, show them they'd done well by me, that my pride was the one they had shaped.

It wasn't until Roi came home, all suited and necktied, that there was any kind of emotional resolution, as though only now could they see me—through him. It hadn't only to do with the way he looked, but what he did. Kellie had run to greet him at the door, and with her he began the long way back to us, through the living room and the two bedrooms, carrying on his habitual banter, lifting her into the air and then setting her down, calling out his pet names: "You midget!" "You munchkin!" "You munchie!" "You munch!"

As the two women watching beside me, together and in the same tone, suddenly uttered that soft, back-of-the-throat, sentimental *aaahhh*. Translating to: This black man loves his child, and teases, is a man the way I know men.

I thought of this visit after reading a review of a book about the Negro Baseball League. A story that needed retelling, the reviewer said. Recalling those women that day I won-

dered how many times since then this story's been told—
and how long before all the scores are finally settled.

That fall of 1960 there was a hint of something new
downtown. It hadn't existed before we'd staked it, and wasn't
yet called counterculture, but it seemed as if our small,
raggedy band of claim to new consciousness was all at once
uncontainable, even though the Court's front room had
probably once held formal receptions. We opened the house
before the paint was even dry: Allen and Peter, helping with
preparations, had brought along Peter's brother Lafcadio,
who lacquered the front door over and over for hours before
we found him. People at the party that night kept coming
to me with murder in their eyes reflected in the red enamel
on their clothes. What could I do? They came and went,
then and from then on. Some I never knew, but we were
the place to pass through, paint and all.

The bourgeois bohemians came for the funk but hated to
part with the structure. One of these, Roi's fancy that fall,
appeared at the house one evening dragging a large, headless
doll she'd found in the street. It was very naked and sexless.
"Isn't it *bizarre!*" she said. Modest Roi's response was a nervous
smile. Joel Oppenheimer, in another conversation nearby,
suddenly turned to this woman, referring to her suburban
Long Island home. "Like they do in Long Beach, where
you're from," he said.

"Not Long Beach, you mean Great Neck," she protested.

Joel, from Yonkers, didn't know much about Long
Island class distinctions. "Great Neck, Long Beach, what's
the difference?" he said with a shrug.

"What's the *difference!*" sputtered Miss Bohemish. "Why,
only—only about a million *dollars!*"

Everyone booed. She was terribly confused, standing

there with her doll. I tried to catch Roi's eye but he was embarrassed and left the room.

Mounted on our building, just above the store, was a metal sign that still bore the name of the departed shoeman. One dead of night, to celebrate Fidel Castro's first UN visit, Roi and a friend hung over the narrow wrought-iron balcony outside our front windows, and painted a new sign in two-foot-high black letters: CUBA SI, YANQUI NO.

Threatening words for those times, they predicted a world at which we're still looking. The Beats, remembered as apolitical, were simply a *growing* consciousness. This is Allen Ginsberg's journal entry of November 1, 1960: "Now that the Congo is independent how come Nelson Rockefeller campaigning for president owns 22½ percent controlling interest in Universal Mines in Katanga?"

Below the metal sign was another prediction, on the Profesora's window under her name: *Le Dirá Todo Lo Que Desea Saber*—She Will Tell You All You Want to Know. But the next day no one who passed confused politics with prophecy, and by nightfall an angry crowd had torn down the sign. Twisted, defaced, for a week it lay like a warning on the sidewalk.

Down the hall from *Partisan*'s rooms on Union Square, a woolens jobber was closing his office. For several years we'd said hello in the elevator, and he had once commented on a dress I'd made. Now here he was in the doorway with a box of foot-square samples, a fine, thick, plushy grade, every one a different shade. "You could find a way to use these, probably," he said. Although I doubted this, I thanked him and dragged the heavy box home and stuck it in a corner.

But he proved to be right. When my winter coat fell apart I made a forty-square poncho, sort of South American biblical, long and wide and warm. Roi's response to it, remarked to someone else, and not without a certain pride, was: "Weird chick."

I had this on my back and a grocery bag in my arms the evening I came home and found him with Allen, Joel, Fee, and some others, as well as two tall fair strangers introduced as Edward Dorn and his wife, Helene. Ed, a former Black Mountain student now living in Santa Fe, had come to New York to read at the 92nd Street Y, which was having an avant-garde poetry series. He and Roi had been corresponding. Raised on midwestern farms, Ed wrote about the West with insight and compassion, I thought, and I had recently asked Philip Rahv to consider some of his stories for *Partisan*. He was a handsome man, with a bony, focused look and a clear sense of his physical self, very elegant in a white raw silk jacket. Helene was beautiful too, one of those extraordinary-looking Nordic women, square-shouldered and nearly as tall as her tall husband, and she *stood* tall. But like Ed she had none of beauty's reserve or coldness, there was nothing distant or withdrawn about her; it was she, in fact, who took the grocery bag from my arms as I struggled out from under my poncho.

"Did you *make* that?" she asked, and then reached a hand to the fabric when I said I had.

"Helene made *this*," Ed said proudly, thumbing the lapels of his jacket, and then opening it to display a perfect, hand-finished lining.

Dapper Roi, who was standing beside him, turned for a closer inspection. "Jeez," he said enviously, and then cutting his eyes at me: "I wish someone would make *me* a jacket!"

I just laughed along with everyone else and shook my head because all of us—including Roi—knew I did enough for him as it was. Anyway I'd recognized a finer hand than mine, but Helene seemed to take her skills as well as her good looks in stride. Her face was buried in the grocery bag.

"Do I smell *bagels* in here?" she said. "You can't get *bagels* in Santa Fe, New Mexico!"

So the two of us, having made acquaintance *through work* rather than simply *as wife*, withdrew to the kitchen and then went out with Kellie, and eventually—though not immediately—I learned all about Helene, born Helmers in Duluth. She'd wanted to paint, but in the forties lucky girls married early. So the War Bond Queen moved up in the world, to the big house on the hill, had a son the first year, then a daughter, then left her wealthy husband to paint again, and almost too soon, it seemed, took up with Ed. "There was a moment," she told me. "I was turning to the stove with a pot in my hand, and I thought, Oh no, I'm doing this again. But I was so in love. . . ."

Then she and Ed had a son and went to Black Mountain, with the three children, where she painted when she could but it was Ed for whom they had the tuition, and anyway Helene could type and edit and sew as well as paint, and there were the children. . . .

In a 1959 *Partisan* article about Allen Ginsberg and the Beats, the critic Diana Trilling had complained of the "girls." She didn't find us pretty, and hadn't liked our legs at all. "So many blackest black stockings," she wrote with distaste.

I never expected then that only a year or so later, at a party in the Hotel Chelsea, I would meet the writer Mary McCarthy, who also published in *Partisan*, and that she would say, smiling, "I like your stockings." Or that I wouldn't be able to resist adding, after I'd thanked her, that she could buy them on Fourteenth Street, at the Bargain Hosiery Center next to the Catholic Church.

It was in front of this store that Helene and I stopped to look at one of those tiny mannequins, sort of a predecessor to Barbie, which was dressed in black stockings and featured

in the window. The store was crowded. It felt odd to have
so prompted the culture, to have many other women want
to seem to *be* you, whatever they thought you were. I turned
to Helene and shrugged. Both of us were wearing black
stockings, of course, but so was an old woman coming from
Mass. Helene was thirty-three years old and for a decade
had lived in remote places, sometimes under makeshift
circumstances, often where merely the mention of art, the
suggestion of "new," was suspect. I watched her check out
the crowd, the mannequin, my legs, her own. Then she
threw her head back and laughed—a big, hearty, gratifying
sound.

"*Bohemia*, momma," she said. Several heads turned.

I loved her at once.

From Santa Fe the Dorns went to Pocatello, Idaho, where
Ed taught a class at a small state college. They lived on a
mountainside, in a borrowed, fixed-up chicken coop, and
began a magazine called *Wild Dog*; Helene did some covers.
In letters she sent me sagebrush, and stories of moose in the
yard, and herbs and flowers her children had picked to be
sent "to your new friend in New York."

I had never liked keeping a journal, gave it up finally,
and thought I would never write prose. But letters were
different. I wrote long, detailed, continued accounts, and
sent them with bargain remnants from the bins at Paterson
Silks. I said whatever came to mind. What remained unsaid—
undiscovered, undone—is equally important, now, from this
long distance. There was a faith between myself and Helene;
we knew that what was incomplete still compelled us, and
hid the same shame at having abandoned it. Abandoned is
not the word, though; there's an old kitchen way to say what
we did: you bury your talent in a napkin.

Sometimes we threw vast sums of money to the wind
and called each other up, but mostly we wrote. Long past
midnight, having been absorbed for hours with trying to *tell*,

I'd be conscious suddenly, and almost surprised to see the dark shapes of the poverty trees at the window. Something in language went, now, where nothing else could go. So I owe it to Dear Helene, my fellow tailor (and eventual sculptor), that I ever left the Singer and took up the pen.

13

There's a tale Roi liked to tell about his mother, in a store one day when a white woman asked the clerk for some "nigger toes." Roi's mother stepped up to the woman. Conversation among the customers stopped. This was in Newark during the forties, Gramma was in her thirties; pictures show her in smart hats, looking directly at the camera. I can imagine her quiet, authoritative tone, sarcastic only at the edges, as, taking her sweet time, she said, to this by now red-faced woman: "Madam, those are . . . *Brazil nuts.*"

Sometimes, telling the story, Roi would beef up the

tension and play it out, give his mother a more aggressive response like a long harangue, or have her swing a pocketbook at the woman's head. (She told me herself that nothing else happened, only a stiff, shamed silence until she left.) But the point, as in other stories told to me, was simply to be on the case, never to let the struggle go, the same position I'd been taught as a Jew. It was not to *propose* the violent solution—violence being the other side's tactic. Violence had driven Roi's family north. He was named—Everett LeRoi— for Thomas Everett Russ, his mother's father, a "race man" (militant), who'd lost a business to arson in Alabama before coming to Newark, where he kept a store and worked for the Board of Elections. His death—a streetlight just happened to fall on his head—was an early grief in Roi's life, the subject of his first story, published in *Yugen 2,* "Suppose Sorrow Was A Time Machine?"

From his father Roi had the rest of his name and another story, its locale the moviehouse in Hartsville, South Carolina, where Coyt Leroy, age fifteen, was ordered to leave for eating peanuts in the Jim Crow section. The manager, a white boy even younger than he, grabbed his collar and tried to drag him from his seat. "I just *had* to hit him then," was how Granddaddy told it. Retelling the story Roi would draw out the "had" into multicolored syllables, the very *sound* of honorable compulsion, *ha-a-e-ea-ad.* But in 1927 whether you had to or not you didn't knock a white boy down. Coyt was sent to live with his married sister in Newark.

My own mother, strong on the idea of service to the race, was weaker on political risk. Walking with her in late thirties Brooklyn, I'd once seen people carrying placards I couldn't yet read. "What is it?" I asked. "Strike," she said, and never another word of explanation.

By 1960 new groups in the South were actively recruiting and training their members—black and white—in the tactics of nonviolent confrontation, but New York was still a quiet world without buttons or T-shirts, the only sticker you put on the car was AAA. The United States was just beginning its campaign of threat against Cuba. After his essay was published, Roi was contacted by an organization called the Fair Play for Cuba Committee. We decided to demonstrate with them at the UN, and recalling that picket line in the thirties I wanted to take Kellie, and *explain*. Roi was for it. But who would carry her wiggly twenty pounds? Only the handle of the stroller folded, but we struggled it into a cab and finally arrived on the line that had begun to circle Ralph J. Bunche Memorial Park, a tiny sliver of land the size of a couple of limos.

It was a cool, dry fall day. Beyond the UN's formal plaza, the East River moved and shone in the sun. An amazingly ordinary background, I thought, to the unreal menace of the scene. There were a dozen mounted police to contain the twenty-five marchers. In due time a crowd gathered. The horses seemed nervous, the police kept moving and turning, reining cowboy-style. After a while one of them stopped me. "You can't walk around with that," he said, pointing to the stroller.

"Why not?" I asked.

"It's not . . . safe," he said.

But I was on the sidewalk, just like everyone else, with the stroller right in front of me. I stood my ground. The picket line stopped.

"Go on," he said. "I said it wasn't safe."

"Are you worried about my kid or your horse?" I said.

The cop sawed at the bit and his horse began flinging its head and stepping. By this time Roi had arrived.

Years later, at all the Vietnam War protests, where babies were such a common sight, I'd remember my angry frustration that day, parked on a bench, with my bewildered daughter in her stroller, watching everyone else march around us.

Some days are like roots. Like Saturday, December 16, 1960. In the afternoon we went to the Judson Church, to a wedding performed by the Reverend Howard Moody, who led demonstrations in Washington Square, married interracial couples, offered space to experimental art, brought into being the Judson Dance Group, the Judson Poets Theater, etc. The role of the church in the arts went on from there.

The groom, a good friend of ours, was another man in a new direction. In the midst of abstraction, Bob Thompson painted figures—eerie, vital men, women, birds, and beasts, in vivid landscapes based on classical models, familiar stories flung into vision again. At twenty-five, from Louisville, he already had the art world's attention: like Roi he'd placed at the avant-garde heart an original, contemporary black consciousness. I'd watched him paint; he worked fast, sure-handed, as if forcing the issue of representation. Bob put race and sex in his paintings, and his own round, dark face—on the body of a large, insistent-looking bird and under the porkpie hat he always wore. After Lester Young, you had to be pretty sure of yourself to wear a porkpie.

Bob's bride, Carol Plenda, was a clothing designer who shared a shop with her sisters Elaine and Kathy. We always thought of the three of them together, as "the Plendas," though each was distinct in face and figure, a redhead, a brunette, and a blonde. They'd come to New York from Ohio, and their shop—also called Plenda—was a crowded little East Sixth Street storefront, where they cut and sewed knitted fabrics, plain T-shirts and skirts and pants with elasticized waists, the prototype of soft, comfortable, interchangeable clothing sans zipper or button. Each Plenda must have seen herself in the one set of patterns they used, as anyone could wear their clothes, which would be copied and altered year after year while remaining the same, woman unbound: the city girl pulls on her warm-up, the Midwest matron drives to work with her ample legs relaxed and spread in her polyester pantsuit.

Someone took a picture of Kellie that evening, among all the grown-up feet at the wedding party, seventeen months to the very day and stuffing her mouth with cake. Beside her, on the paint-splashed floor of Bob's Clinton Street loft, is an array of paper cups. That's her stash, she's claimed her space. In the decade to come there'll be many more like her, bridging the generation gap, wearing "Kids Are Only Newer People" buttons. But here, in 1960, hers are the only little hightop shoes in sight.

That night, I'm the only one still awake. Warming my back at the space heater near my desk. All the lights are off, and outside the window the high December full moon is grinning, as if it has put one over on me, which it has. I'd made a dress for the wedding, a red brocade in a new, wider shape; and now there's no denying my too-tight belly and tender breasts. Which came first? Did a pregnant woman design the dress? I pull out the front to see how many months it might comfortably cover, suddenly wishing I could will this into existence at once. Like Bob Thompson painting his brown and yellow and orange people. Mothering one has piqued my interest in a second. It's growing realer by the minute. I'm counting the months on my fingers. A hot summer baby, two years plus three months younger than Kellie. This will thrill her. And Roi? I thought he'd be okay.

Moonlight defines the familiar, his shape under the bedclothes, her small, exhausted, satisfied form. I imagine another like these two, and then it's as if my heart were actually widening, and spreading, and then with a sudden, sharp, familiar thrust it pulses into the swollen weight of my breasts.

△   △   △

Roi raised no objection, nor did he volunteer much comment, as if this were just what happened to you in your life. Though he liked catching up to family men he knew. In Newark the Joneses agreed that the time was right. Roi and his sister were also two years apart. Gramma said, with her sly grin, "I was wondering when you'd get to work on that."

My own mother—once again—wept.

Soon, fighting fatigue, there were times I wanted to weep too. *Partisan*, though short of stories, rejected Ed Dorn's. "Too much like Kerouac," said Philip Rahv, waving off further discussion. (Untrue, untrue!) Roi was out early and home late, closing the bar, or the door of the woman from Great Neck, or tenacious Diane Di Prima, who believed herself at the head of the lengthening line. All my former tolerance seemed gone. I was angry most of the time. I dragged across Fourteenth Street in my coat of many colors, physically larger but feeling as if I were shrinking. The hospital gave me iron, the belly grew into the dress.

One winter night, with some other friends, we had dinner at Basil and Martha King's new loft, downtown near the docks on Ferry Street, where I used to visit the man with the motor scooter. With dessert there was marijuana, newly known as grass and easier than ever to get. Around midnight, after falling asleep for a time, I opened my eyes to see Roi in a corner, slow-dancing with another contender. She was smiling at him, the way everyone did; he had nothing but admiration and love from all sides. But all he ever had for me was a frown: I'd cheated him again, his weird chick was just a pregnant woman. Still, I didn't have to watch him perform. I grabbed my coat and ran downstairs to the cobblestone street, where, in place of my past romance, there was now a hulking, cement, post office receiving station. It had to be a comment on me.

When Roi arrived at home I told him, in a loud,

screaming drench of tears, while he sat speechless in a corner, that he was making me unhappy and ought to check himself out, because having all these women was *thing*amatizing him, couldn't he *see?*

A day later, unburdened, I felt better. But he'd decided to move out. He told me this in the kitchen, after I came home from work. It was all arranged, he was taking A.B. Spellman's apartment. "So you won't be unhappy," he said. I was amazed, devastated. In the middle of cooking. He was ashamed then, and upset, and he left. I spent half the night on a letter, repeating where I thought he was at, and inviting him back for watermelon. When he returned he read it, then turned away. "Why *must* you?" I asked.

"[Miss Bohemish] is a beautiful woman," he said.

Is that all? The world is *full* of beautiful women. "I'm beautiful too!" I shrieked, suddenly an inconsolable baby, "I'm beautiful too! You said so yourself! I'm beautiful too!"

Next week, in a nightmare, I'm yelling his name. Around me a crowd is roaring a garble of praise, or is it derision, there's talk of an execution, it's to be Roi—my god, I see him now, on a *scaffold*. But no one's holding him—I scream and scream, the warnings tear out of me like fire, burning my throat—run, Roi, *Roi, run!* I wake to the sound of my voice. In the half-dark, March wind flying through the rooms. But the dream hangs on. In a poem he'd once referred to me as the biblical witch of Endor, and it was death, after all, that she foresaw. One day he would write about another separation between us, a play I always called Roi's nightmare. I never told him mine.

The white South showed its face on Kellie's second birthday, May 16, 1961. The Congress of Racial Equality (CORE) had organized a "Freedom Ride"—for the right to the bus, the restroom, and the restaurant in the terminal. There were shocking, blatant brutalities, burning buses, blood. A new, angry, viable politics, a coalescing vision called the civil rights movement.

My own life was reduced to economics. Without Roi I'd have to cross the border, get a "real," uptown job. But he had never changed his address. He came daily to pick up his mail, invited me to his nearby apartment for lunch. Got embarrassed when I wouldn't go to bed.

One evening that spring, wandering the streets with Kellie asleep in the stroller, I stopped at the Cedar and found—for the first time—someone else from Far Rockaway High School. Her name was Helen Wildenberg and she'd even been in my class. Now she was an editor married to the painter Mario Irizarry. She was terribly excited; I was a first for her too. She asked, "How did you ever get out of there?"

Trading stories I stayed out later than usual and ran into Roi on University Place. He was surprised. He said, "What are you doing out here?" It seemed to be the same question as Helen's. I just looked at him and shook my head and left him standing on the corner. I'd relinquished myself, it seemed, had given him power over me. And now to my shame I was caught in a wary, threatened, indecisive present. I'd become obedient.

In June he brought me, fresh off the press, his first book, *Preface To A Twenty Volume Suicide Note*, which Totem had published in conjunction with Corinth Books, owned by Eli and Ted Wilentz of the Eighth Street Bookshop. "This book is Hettie's" read the dedication, and below it a poem from the Sanskrit, in part: "Had I gone between [the leopards] then / and torn them asunder by their manes / I would have run less risk / Than when I passed in my boat / And saw you . . . / Ready to dive and kindle the river . . ."

Reading this made me feel worse, much much worse. "Why didn't you change it," I said bitterly.

Roi and Diane—mostly Diane, who owned the mimeo-graph—were mailing a sheet called *The Floating Bear*, its purpose to publish new work faster than the quarterly *Yugen*. Its frequent appearances were ideal for messages. Next issue there was a quote from a slave narrative, about not being able to "break" love. "After you lub you lub," it said. "She stick like tar."

Now he's on the couch in the living room, his face with its bones and planes all contorted, his arm around me like an awkward boyfriend. "I want to come home," he whispers, "but Diane told me you went to bed with A.B. and I couldn't stand that."

Me? When his affairs were public, and he'd abandoned me for his right to them! This man is *crazy!* Are all men crazy?

Besides, I *didn't!* I almost did—and what if I had? But I *didn't!*

So here he is with a poem about how he still loves me. Head inclined, lips compressed, he hands it to me and stands beside me as I read it. And he knows I'm a sucker for words. We don't say anything, we just stand there, close together in that quiet, original certainty of ours, and let the feeling ride the air between us.

I went to his next reading, in the White Whale on Tenth Street, a new jazz/poetry place. It was funky, with a high, stamped-tin ceiling. Wooden floor, folding chairs, a fish on the wall. Most of the other faces were familiar. Under red and purple flowered curtain fabric, my belly was an eight-month bloom. Someone called my name, loud and pleased, into the room.

△ △ △

In the steaming middle of the summer, at an enormous fund-raiser party for CORE, we danced for most of the night. There was a guy on the scene, a painter known as Big Ray Johnson, who had not got his name for nothing, and I was so happy that even though nearly nine months gone I tired him out. "Mama," he said, sweating, "I can't wait to dance with you *after* you've had that baby!"

The day our second daughter was born I got home from work at six. Labor started at midnight. Someone rushed Roi home on a motorcycle from Dillons, the new hangout two blocks north of the Cedar, and luckily closer than Pennsylvania, since this girl took barely two hours, a hint of how fast she moves today. Unlike Kellie she was yelling her head off, which did not stop the resident doctor from dumping her onto the cold metal arm of the table. But they hadn't had time to tie me—or reckoned with my agility—and howls of protest rose as I turned in the stirrups and grabbed her.

"Pretty spry, ain't you," said a disapproving voice behind me, but they let me hold the little, bawling thing. It was August 15, 1961, nine months short a day since we'd met. I felt as if I knew her. We'd been through rough times together, and could speak as friends. "It's okay," I whispered. "Now that you're here it'll all be much better, I'm sure, don't cry, it's okay, I promise."

14

TOTEM PRESS   *324 East Fourteenth St.   New York 3, N.Y.*

October 21, 1961

Dear Helene,

Glub, she said as her head came up for the first time since August. It's midnight and I think I've finally caught Symphony Sid, although this radio is prone to stick on less desirable stations. My desk is full so I've taken over Roi's study for the evening— he's out reading revolutionary Spanish poetry, with

Paul Blackburn and a visiting Dominican, who with God's help and a few others intends to overthrow the Trujillos one day, amen. I have some hot coffee and a warm sweater and feel awfully safe from the cold, newyorkwet out there. From the kitchen just now I could see a Puerto Rican party across the way, everyone dressed and having a ball with the shades up, which reminds me of how much a city girl I am, to love this place and this particular brand of safety, the jazz and the crumbly walls. And now a brief bit of the old from Wilbur de Paris, the man just said (no, he's not Sid at all). Once I loved a banjo player, who brought home the clarinetist Omer Simeon, who played with Wilbur de Paris and left his umbrella at my apartment. Later the banjoist, o unhip soul, played dixieland with Turk Murphy. All this before everything now, my pretty babies, my errant/sometimes but often lovely husband. Everything is really OK.

Let me tell you about Lisa Victoria Chapman Jones, said the fond mother, gloating. She has large brown slanted eyes, skin the color of rare clay, not much hair, a beautiful mouth usually open. Better than anyone else she seems to like Kellie, who aside from some standard shows is really coming through it well. Since everyone knows that this is really *her* baby, anyway.

I've stopped working! (!!!) Again, from *Partisan*, unemployment for six months, more money per week than I had after paying Miss Bailey. . . .

I think Roi has already written to Ed about his arrest on Wednesday for sending obscenity through the mails in *The Floating Bear*. Wow, was I panicky at first. Three charming creatures, an FBI man and two postal inspectors, came to the door, quarter to eleven in the morning. He's under arrest, they say.

For what says I all atremble, hair standing on end. Wake up, *Leee*-roy, says the FBI, shaking him (he was fast asleep) and me all the time yelling what for, I have a right to know what he's being arrested for, until the motherfucker tells me "shut up or I'll arrest you too." Roi sat up in bed pretty calmly there in his underwear and said what am I being arrested for and the guy finally spit out the obscenity charge. I was really relieved, it could have been any one of a number of things, you know. . . . And then the bastards grabbed our water pipe and took it to be analyzed, Roi told them a friend had sent it from Tangiers. They still have it and I half expect them to raid us and search, though if they haven't by now I guess they've got better things to do than hang us for possession. Anyway we haven't got anything, it's just not safe these days, not in this house. So I spent all day calling the newspapers, lawyers, people-to-help, etc. and now we have an expensive, unnecessary thing to deal with. At a very bad time, too, since we're being evicted and have to find a place to live soon, have no money, the usual. The Court's going to be renovated and three (*three!*) apartments to be made out of it. . . .

Happily, though, in the midst of all these crises and changes I feel pretty strong and capable. To-morrow Robert Creeley is reading. I've never met him and I really look forward to it. The news about his daughter was so terrible, something I can't talk about, that kind of injustice, the death of a child, oh.

I am looking at, in any order, pictures of, no I guess it's left to right, Lester Young, Pocahontas, what's-his-name-er-Ezra Pound, Erich von Stroheim, Jones by Dawson, Allen Ginsberg in front of the Parthenon, W. C. Fields, and a number of unnamed gods (Eastern and Western), the first page of a play called *The Death of the Lone Ranger*, a letter from Olympia Press, and the October page of a Japanese calendar. Then Norman Bluhm's cover painting for *Yugen* 7 with an overlay of all sorts of printing instructions like crop and bleed, and a reproduction of some Florentine sculpture from the fifteenth century, titled, of course, "The Inferno According to Dante." All this in one corner, my immediate view, all of it on the wall. Roi says in one of his poems, "You are / as any other sad man here/ american." But what is that? We're all compounded of so much, in our funny heads and treasures, we Americans here and you in Idaho, in between us that vast never-never, is it one big gas station yet?

And there goes Lisa. All the mothers in the world are up, it's 2 A.M. Write soon, I'm anxious to hear from you.

At the curb on a corner of Fourteenth and First, late one fall afternoon. It's beginning to rain. Hurrying people eddy around me, I'm a convoy in a traffic dilemma: I've got a baby carriage on the sidewalk, a shopping cart piled with clean laundry in the street, and a fallen sheet getting mucky in the gutter. I hate to let go of the carriage because it's collapsible and tends to fulfill this function, making it something to operate more than just steer, and thus requiring sensitivity, careful attention, and quick, firm decision—from me, like everything else in my life. Lisa, for one: she was propped on a pillow under the hood, but slid down on the trip up the curb. Now I hear her insistent *wah wah*, which I know won't stop of itself, since she's the kind who must *see*— everything, at all times. Often, to make dinner, in these days before infant seats, I tie her onto me with pieces of fabric.

It's easier. But is it? Experience distances, leads you to the clean, dry air of generalization. I'd be the first to say (when not stuck in the rain) that such a will as Lisa's is nothing to thwart, that I'd encourage it in anyone, and obviously did in Kellie, who, in a seat clamped across the top of the carriage, has twisted around to offer advice, further tipping our tenuous balance and also—incidentally?—her hard shoes are an inch from her sister's head.

I'm not a convoy, I'm a thrumming blinking bleating switchboard.

Given my attachment to the living cargo, these adorable small ganglia of human complication, even though one is yelling at me, and I'm about to yell at the other, I let go not of them but of the shopping cart. By now the sheet is nothing I can put on my bed tonight. The wasted effort, the extra quarter to dry it pass my mind in a wave of disgust, I hate *applying* myself to it again. Nevertheless, clutching the carriage handle like an unstable ballet barre I plié toward it, when suddenly—

Just under my outstretched arm, the veined, spotted hands of an elderly woman appear. Snatching the sheet she flips it onto the stack of damp clothes, brushes it off, and then with surprising strength jams the stack into the cart and hauls the whole thing onto the sidewalk. She's wearing an old blue coat with military buttons, and above her beautiful Irish face her white hair is a thick ropy pile. She's dismissing my thanks, too, because there's something bitter on her mind. "The men, they don't know about this," she says. "They don't know and they don't care to know, them with their lives, their damned *lives*." And then she's gone.

At the northern tip of East River Park there's an overgrown quarter acre with some benches facing the water and a neglected, sinking monument to the dead of World War II. In 1961, when Stuyvesant Towners never ventured south, and people from the Jacob Riis housing project seldom went north, the solitude was impressive.

I was there one day, sitting apart from the children in order to pay attention to myself, impossible in their immediate presence: if they demanded they also seduced, like the TV that captures because it's on. We'd left Roi at home, typing in his windowless box of a room. When I'd looked in to say good-bye he was grinning. Through Joyce, who was now working at the publisher William Morrow, he'd just met an editor with whom he'd discussed a book about the blues, a critical study of the music, its antecedents, contexts, the lives of the people who made it. The editor thought the project exciting and novel, not least because it would be the first full-length work on the subject by a *Negro*. Negroes were now newsworthy. A trend had been spotted. Book sales could be predicted. Joyce was sure Roi's proposal would go through, that it was just a matter of his writing it. All week he'd been bouncing his chair and stamping his feet and yelling "Yeah! Yeah!"—the way he'd always applaud a good solo (you can hear him on some of the Monk records made at the Five Spot). Like the kids he was a bundle of jumpy good humor, demanding instant gratification. Yesterday evening, while I was bathing Kellie, he'd come dashing into the bathroom with a poem. "Look at this! Read this!" he cried. I dried my hands and grabbed it—why not?

Today, everything in the landscape seemed in an act of relation, reflected in and reflecting. Shadows of trees dappled the water; the river, refracting sun, played on the tree trunks. The children were part of the pattern too, their eyes were on each other. And what, then, of me? Would there ever be a way to balance Roi?

I began to try to sort myself out. I'd graduated *Partisan*. I'd finished bearing children. I was growing out my hair, and my head had outgrown what my hand could sew. Life as wife and mother was fine because of other pleasures—the unemployment insurance in my pocket, the promise, from friends in publishing, of free-lance editorial work. *Yugen* 7 was out, a sixty-six-page issue; Totem Press had eleven titles. These were now printed with money advanced by Corinth, but we—mostly me—still ran our business (when Ted Wilentz had first offered to back us, he'd joked to Roi that he was giving him money only because he trusted his wife).

Still I knew what was missing, and what that white-haired woman on the corner had meant. All told, I was an energetic young person of twenty-seven, serving others.

The monument to the dead of World War II brought to mind my first love, my second-youngest uncle, fixer of my father's comb-case machine. Though he'd married and moved to the Bronx, the telegram announcing his death in the war came to Laurelton; arriving home from Newark one night we found it under the door: *We regret to inform you . . .* I was ten when he died, but dead he refused to die, and in my mind descended again and again the stairway where I'd seen him last. At seventeen, desperate to set him to rest, I wrote him a poem. It worked.

Since then only the future had ever obsessed me, as if art were not work but a simple act of faith, and only by *seeing* myself at it would I ever make it happen. Though I admired poets like Denise Levertov and Barbara Guest, I felt I could never write like they did, with astonishing, sophisticated metaphor, and anyway I only wanted to write like William Carlos Williams, with tones and repetitions, a kind of melody line, the language equivalent to Miles's pretty, ambivalent notes. Like Creeley's:

> *Let me be my own fool*
> *of my own making, the sum of it*
> *is equivocal.*

Kellie was calling. "Mommy!"

I went to look. Lisa was moving every muscle, as if jumping or running, and her mouth was working too, like "Wow! Wow! Wow!"—and all because of the same reflections I'd noticed, the riverlight on the trees. Kellie, perceiving this response as opinion, and thus some progress in consciousness, exclaimed, proudly, "They look *good* to her!"

Only the verb in this sentence differs from a line in a poem by Williams. That night—reconvinced—I started a book for children. I figured I'd just go back to where I left off, before the kids, Totem, *Yugen*, Roi. . . . I thought it would be good training, and felt stubborn about the method, even if writers were supposed to have more on their minds, and even if Gregory Corso, continuing a current argument in *Yugen* 7, had suggested that the idea of writing nursery rhymes would produce a "stark" poetry.

Inevitably we all write for our children or end up talking to ourselves, but the book I began remained unfinished; ten years would pass before my first published children's book; and in thinking that I'd commenced with myself, I was—extremely as usual—mistaken. I even lost the manuscript, probably in the pile on my desk, most of which weren't mine during this time. Publishers paid me to read Beckett, Burroughs, Marguerite Duras, Fanon, Genet, and many more. I thought about all of it. But my feelings—with never anything literary to them and all I ever wanted to write about—were left tangled for lack of time, like the long hair I grew but then twisted up carelessly. There are different reasons for silences, but the Russian poet Marina Tsvetayeva, describing her own, came closest to mine: "It's precisely for feeling that one needs time, and not for thought." Anyway, now I think I'm lucky to have, from Fourteenth Street, the one poem that mattered, which offered at last what the gypsies could never have seen—a future I'd invented and therefore couldn't disappoint—the rest of my life from prophetic twenty-seven:

I've been alive since thirty-four
and I've sung every song
since before the War

Will the press of this music
warp my soul
till I'm wrinkled and gnarled
and old and small—

A crone in the marshes
singing and singing

A crone in the marshes singing
and singing

and singing
and singing
and singing
and singing
and singing

15

The day the kitchen ceiling fell I came home to a pile of plaster and lathe and a dent in the Gilbert Sorrentinos' washing machine, a luxury loan while they went on an extended tour out west. Roi, the broom clenched in his hands, was alternately sweeping and stopping to glare at the two-foot hole. "I've already called the city," he said. "They're going to send an inspector." He gave me a satisfied look.

"An inspector?" I said. After the FBI, I didn't like the idea. But Roi did, and the ceiling became his issue. Everyone got a look at the mess and the story of how, when the noise of it started, he'd come flying out of his study with the only weapon he could find—a wooden coat hanger!

I was less concerned with the ceiling than the washing

machine, the damage to which, though negligible, proved something of an omen, since soon we heard that the Sorrentinos themselves had split up. Elsene, taking their two children, had run away with a friend of a friend. . . . Gil returned to New York alone. When he came to see us he wandered into the kitchen and stood leaning sadly on the machine, as though for comfort. "Why did she do it, Hettie?" he asked.

Having barely learned to ask the question I was nowhere near the answer. I realized how little I knew of Elsene. She was pretty, and seemingly lighthearted, a woman who liked to dance. During our communal weekends we'd confided some, mainly about birth control problems. All I'd ever seen of her married life was the basement they lived in, far out in Brooklyn. Elsene stayed home with her daughter and son. She never spoke of ambitions. Was she lonely? Was she doing what she'd expected to do? Was it too difficult, living in that cramped place, quieting two little kids so Gil could write? The previous year she'd had an affair with A.B. Spellman. Everyone knew, the way they'd known about Mike and me, Roi and Diane. It was marriage that held all the secrets. In any case, my sympathies lay with the closest victim. I rubbed Gil's shoulder, and told him honestly that I didn't know why she'd done it.

When the inspector arrived, he and Roi stood side by side, gazing steadily upward, as if by intent alone to get through the hole to the cause, the broken pipe in the kitchen upstairs, which belonged to an odd, secretive, overweight group. But effect, not cause, was on Roi's mind. "It could have hurt my *family*," he said to the stout, middle-aged inspector, no doubt a family man himself, who at this nodded gravely. It amused me to hear Roi savor the word, the way it pleased him to use it to prove his point. That protectiveness, with its hint of the proprietary, so obviously had a reverse—what you own you can also give away. But when I was happy, as now, I liked to hear love in it—loyalty not lordship—and anyway I thought Gil's loss had affected Roi, and I felt tender toward him for that. And I certainly didn't mind the rent reduction, after the inspection, or the fact that in protest we paid nothing, since no one ever came to plug up the hole. It was this that had led to the eviction proceedings. We were holding out for moving money, rumored to be something close to a thousand dollars.

Rolling in prospects, we hosted Thanksgiving. The setup was two tables end to end covered with sheets, as close to a formal dinner as I would get. We were a couple of dozen people, halfway into the food and definitely into the booze when Joel Oppenheimer arrived late yelling for us to come look outside.

We rushed to the front. A long row of double-parked cars filled the street. There were new and old models, two Cadillacs with high fifties fishtails, one of them an amazing, aging lavender. As we crowded the windows a limousine— something you rarely saw then—pulled up in front of the house. "Jesus—look at that *thing*," Roi said. Several women in long dresses climbed out, and then a burly, self-important-looking man. Fielding Dawson was standing beside me. "It must be the king," he said in an awed, tipsy voice. "The king of the gypsies," he whispered, as though that meant every-thing, and then, inspired, waving his glass of bourbon, he announced to the room: "The king . . . of the gypsies . . . is here!"

And, as we later saw from the stoop, set for the king and his elegant tribe was no meager two-together table like ours, but a linen-covered *banquet*, the entire length of the place, laden with food and drink. And after a while—live music!

Much later, coming back from the all-night store with a carton of milk, I ran into Profesora Luz's elder daughter, a thin, pale woman I thought might be the mother of the little boy who lived with them. I'd never determined which of the men I sometimes saw was her husband, or whether she had one. On her days in the window she'd stare right through me, swinging her leg mechanically, as if she were less a person than a requirement, an animated part of the painted sign. Now she'd been transfigured, she was breathless and smiling, and for the first time in my presence a contemporary. "Oh *hello!*" I sang out drunkenly. "Hello," she answered, very softly and guardedly, and that—although we've both been on the Lower East Side for twenty years since—was the only time we ever spoke.

I did speak at Gil and Elsene's divorce trial, though, and so did Roi. We had to swear we'd seen Gil making love, any number of times, with a woman who wasn't his wife. He had agreed to this, the only way to get a New York divorce then. The courtroom was intimidating, the looks we got were like knives, and I hated lying. I said yes to the lawyer's questions about Gil while thinking about Elsene. Roi and I took a taxi home in glum, companionable silence. In my mind the pictures alternated: Elsene lonely in the low-ceilinged basement, Gil with his head on his arms on the washing machine. Which unlike its owners ran on smoothly, despite the surface imperfection. I can't remember now which one of them took it, but we didn't have it long after that.

The newly formed Judson Poets Theater was looking for actresses. "Come be in a play with me," Joyce said over the phone. "There's a part for a comedienne. You've had acting experience. You can do it."

I laughed. With most other people Joyce was reticent, even withdrawn, but toward me she could be bossy. "You can" and "You must" sprinkled her sentences. She'd say amazing things, like "A proper girl should always have a nailbrush."

The play was *The Contest*, by Ursule Molinaro, a one-act

on the Judson's second bill of avant-garde theater. For the first production, an enthusiastic group had crowded the choir loft, where the vaulted ceiling made up for the minimal floor space, and the proximity of actor to audience recalled those early, excited café poetry readings. Featured had been Joel's spoof western, *The Great American Desert*, in which Joyce had played a cowgirl—the only female part.

All the characters in *The Contest* were familiar Greek heroines. Joyce was going to be Antigone. I ran to Washington Square and auditioned—feeling suddenly very Jewish and nervous—in a room where the only art on the wall was a crucifix. Larry Kornfeld, the director, offered me the comic role of Ariadne. (Who in legend betrays her father for her lover. I suppose I fit.)

Rehearsals began in December. Vertamae Smart-Grosvenor, who played Cassandra, was a tall, attractive black woman from Philadelphia, with a growing reputation as a cook (among other things she would later write a book called *Vibration Cooking*). She was married to the painter Bob Grosvenor then and they had a daughter. Verta brought Kali, and I brought Kellie, and they bopped around the stage with us. Lisa had to be taken out of her snowsuit and propped. One day she was sleeping, and Washington Square seemed small-town quiet, so I left her in the carriage beside the church steps. Upstairs, though, I had Jewish second thoughts, and after twice flying offstage, and down and up the four flights of stairs, I woke her—and carried her around for the rest of the rehearsal.

"Is fate guilty of your suffering or did you bring tears upon yourselves?" is the question the play poses of its heroines, according to one reviewer, who added: "This is stirring only if one is interested in these antique ladies, which I am not particularly." Sharing this opinion was my husband, who attended neither of the two performances.

When I confronted him he was full of excuses. He hung his head and mumbled. He didn't think the playwright was any good, he said. He thought I was only doing Larry Kornfeld a favor.

What did that matter?

Soon enough I found out where he'd been, having a fling with a new girl in town, ex-wife of a West Coast poet, who'd come for a taste of New York. She called the house looking for him. "Don't call here," I said. "But Roi—" she said. "Call again and I'll fuck up your face," I said, suddenly inspired. She made a little shocked noise in her throat before she hung up and went back to California.

The Contest was the last play Joyce and I were in. That month her novel *Come and Join the Dance* was published by Atheneum, and soon she married James Johnson, who rode her on his motorcycle even in her proper skirts. I baked their wedding cake in five different kinds of pans, cantilevered the layers into one impossible structure, something like marriage itself, and then slathered the thing with chocolate to cover the cracks and the crumbling corners. In the end it looked like a fortress. Sweet, though.

Before we left Fourteenth Street we gave one last party, on New Year's eve, 1962. I heard it was a blast, although I can't say this for sure, for though I was there I wasn't, quite, since I was unintentionally tripping. The use of which word is anachronistic here—the hippies tripped, we just took drugs.

Timothy Leary, then a professor at Harvard, had recently come to town with psilocybin, his new, man-made, still experimental psychedelic. He'd given this magic mushroom to a number of writers including Roi, and like all the ancient druggies of the world had made much of the careful trip setup, specifically sober friends around to calm the willies and guide one on the path. I duly offered my presence. Roi sat beside me, repeating, "No, I can't explain it!" In fact he didn't like the high at all—didn't learn a thing, he said— and never got any more of the stuff. Since you had to be an artist to get some from Leary, I figured I'd find my higher consciousness when I ran into it.

Earlier that New Year's evening I'd taken a more familiar trip, with the children on the bus to Newark. It was snowing heavily and Gramma was late meeting us. I huddled on a deserted corner, holding the bundled-up baby in one arm, hugging the toddler with the other, and trying to generate warmth. Because the roads were bad the return to New York took longer than usual and by the time I got home the party had started. I was much too tired to party, but I changed my clothes and looked around for an "up" so I could.

It took the next generation to prove that speed kills, but like all my friends I took amphetamine when I wanted to. It was useful. Joyce ate half a Dexedrine tablet each night to finish her novel. Roi kept several in his pocket (arrested at a demonstration, he swallowed them *all*). I'd had a good head start from our family doctor in Laurelton, a kind man who loaned me books and gave me Benzedrine for a five-pound weight loss. I was fifteen when I first got this prescription, and the racing heart was a small price for the magically sharpened concentration.

But all I wanted now was to stay at the party. It was getting toward midnight, and the crowd was passing champagne as I searched for someone I knew who usually had a supply. I'd fancied this man, one night, before I was married. Now he went into his pocket as soon as I opened my mouth. I never dreamed there were men on this earth who didn't know "up" from "out." Nor did I know that psilocybin was out of the lab and on the market. Anyway, I just heave ho and swallowed a sugar cube full of it.

Roi was furious. He couldn't stand this man, of course (although he later allowed him to direct one of his plays). He leaned over me in the bathroom, asking rhetorical questions while I vomited. "How could you take it from

157

him?" "How could you be so *stupid?*" I was not prepared to debate. There was no heat in the bathroom. I stood shivering in the short, thin dress I'd intended to dance in. "Just one favor," I gasped. "I know you can't stay with me, but—bring me the quilt off our bed."

"There are *people* sitting on the bed, I can't just rip the fucking quilt off," he said. He took me into the study and then went out to host the party.

I sat down to wait for whatever came next. There wasn't any heat in this room either. If he really loved me, I thought, he'd have thrown the people off the bed and brought me the goddamn quilt. That was the trouble with him—appearances counted. But I *know* that, I thought. I didn't ask myself why only the quilt would do—why I didn't just get my coat from the closet. I began to shiver the way I'd only seen animals shiver, until one violent convulsion sent the wheeled chair out from under me, and me to the floor in front of what I hadn't even noticed, an enormous pile of coats, the topmost of which still glistened with snow. With a cry of relief I burrowed in, under all that steamy, human-smelling wool, and lay still until the shivering stopped. I felt warm and relaxed and sublimely lucid. Several people came in and threw their coats on the pile. No one noticed me. Well, I thought comfortably, I'll be fine. It came to me that the quilt had been on my childhood bed in Laurelton, and I felt pleased to have done with it, if indeed it had been a symbol, and thanked Roi for inadvertently pointing this out. Then I felt glad to have done without whatever other comfort he might have offered, as though I had solved an intricate problem in self-sufficiency. It's all about improvisation, I thought.

Suddenly outside the room all of downtown Manhattan began to lurch and roar and then dance as the clock moved past twelve. I climbed out and opened the door. The whirling mob seemed first like a Breughel, then a Bosch, but it still wasn't anything astonishing. Then the walls began to yaw and stretch. Never mind this shit, I thought. No wonder Roi hadn't liked it. I went back inside and lay down in the wooly womb and closed my eyes, floating weightless in warm space, thinking of the cold night outside, of standing in the snow holding the children. A vision of us grew, contained and enclosed, as if we were inside an old-fashioned paperweight. Hands in my head reached out and shook it, and the snow fell all over us, but we stood smiling and warm. This is how fact becomes fiction, I thought. I began to hallucinate beautiful, complicated colors. Well, I'd rather be dancing but I guess I need the rest, I thought finally. I was sound asleep when they pulled the last coat off.

Rumpled and reborn, I emerged to confront the morning cleanup. The half-dozen people who'd stayed said hello without comment. Roi was mopping the floor. He looked down his nose for a moment, and then went back to the job, with never a question about my experience—since, unlike his, mine had to do with my bad taste in men. I drank some coffee and changed my clothes and then took the subway and the bus to Newark, and made the trip back with my bundled babies. Happy New Year, 1962.

Regarding segregated housing, *de facto* equals *de jure* when you need something quick. Both of us had gone out looking. Basil and Martha's landlord turned me away when I told him I had a black family. Roi, refused by a Village realtor, filed a complaint with a recently established city review board. Complaining did not solve the problem.

But a day or so into the year he came home with news, and that night in bed drew me floor plans, shaping hallways and sets of stairs in the darkness. He was excited, rocking the bed with his gestures, as if he'd already put himself in this place and liked the man he saw there. "It's a house," he said, "a real house, wait till you see. I've got the key, you can go tomorrow, if you like it we can have it."

Profesora Luz had already moved, leaving only her name on the window. What I was to leave on Fourteenth Street was something I'd managed to keep for most of a decade, a head I sculpted in high school that bore a remarkable likeness to Roi, beard and all. My boyfriend then, a ceramist, undertook to glaze it a shiny black when he fired it, to my surprise since I hadn't envisioned the person as any color other than the clay. It was really just one of those things you never mean to keep but can't throw away either. I thought it was strange, the resemblance, and when people asked me who had modeled Roi I used to laugh and say I'd dreamed him.

I did, of course, parts of him anyway, and made him into what he couldn't be, that fictional lover/husband we all expected. Sometimes, contrite, he'd say, "I've failed you again." But I felt he had expectations of me that I hadn't fulfilled, and all we could do was keep trying.

Anyway, he seemed to have a new, hard eye on the future. "Hey," he said, turning to me thoughtfully, "I hope you won't *look* old when you *get* old."

"Hah!" I said. "*I* won't if *you* won't."

COOPER
SQUARE

16

At nine in the morning it seemed less a place to stop than somewhere you'd pass going anywhere else. And it wasn't a square but a long triangle, its base the old brown Cooper Union building, like a hand-tinted rotogravure on the blue winter sky. A mountain of snow from the New Year's storm was piled at the corner of Fifth Street, between me and the Five Spot, which daylight rendered shockingly nondescript. The only other people around were rag-wrapped, grizzled winos straggling up from the Bowery. All I could feel was the age of the place. But the number on the door—27—matched the tag wired to the key I was holding.

I let myself in. The wooden door had a glass pane,

like—what had Roi said—a real house?—well, it was a real door. Inside, steep narrow stairs led to the next two floors and then ended at the top, the floor we'd have, a thick-walled warren where I immediately got lost. Like the rest of the house, it had been empty for years. In the corners of some of the rooms were sections of the narrow pipe once used for gaslight, but none for cooking or heat, in fact it felt colder inside than out. But in the last room I came to, which had brick walls with rough beams and a long, stamped-tin ceiling, there were a couple of chairs and some other evidence of recent squatting—actual, for anyone taller than I, since the roof sloped to a wall only five feet high. Measuring myself against it I found, discarded in a corner, some empty paint tubes, a rolled-up Jasper Johns poster, and—the clincher—a pair of sneakers my size.

Was it only because of plumbing that this room became the kitchen?

Right then I was simply enraptured, as Roi had been, by the idea of life in a skylighted garret. Dashing home to add my *yes* I forgot the key in the real front door, necessitating an immediate change of the lock. But no one minded, there was nothing in the place to steal (I was wearing the sneakers). From Fourteenth Street we'd have to salvage gas heaters, toilet, stove—even the kitchen sink.

Which like me remains on Cooper Square but linked to an earlier time and place. So that tonight, at the dishes, though twice her age I can also see that person I was at twenty-seven, bathing in her kitchen sink, with all of downtown at her back, and the morning sun ablaze in the poverty trees.

Newark
Midnight, March 31, 1962

Dear Helene,

Your letter arrived this morning as I stood in the near 70 degree Cooper Square sunshine watching the bums shake bad winter out of their bones—and there you are still snow-covered. Oh, to fly you all into this hothouse . . .

I'm nearing the end of a six-week sojourn with the kids at Roi's parents, where I landed after we left Fourteenth Street. The new house will be ready soon, but meantime Newark has been pleasant, quiet, televisiony. Granddaddy sings Lisa to sleep with "The Old Gray Goose Is Dead." I've been seeing Roi once a week, it's like having a date, meeting your lover in someone else's apartment. . . . And there he is with no clean underwear complaining to me about it, eating in the Cedar (food is ghastly) and living in Fee Dawson's loft with our two cats stinking up the place.

I was there last night. . . .

When I arrived, Roi wasn't home. Fee was out of town. I settled myself on the stairs outside his door, inhaling the comfort of turpentine and wood, all dressed up in my new old coat from a warehouse on Great Jones Street, around the corner from my new old house. Old clothes, not a new thing, have been changed by a word: *antique.*

I have this coat because Roi has signed with Morrow to write the blues book. He's been turning out a chapter a week for me to edit and retype. I deliver one chapter and pick up another in a worn, brown *Record Changer* envelope. It's beside me now on the step. Its most recent label, one of many, says, Hold for Future Reference.

Enter the late one. I watch him climb the long stairway toward me, he springs up two at a time, grinning. I grin back. Why am I so glad to see him, even after these five years? After lies and infidelities, and other large and small betrayals, hardly discussed, little understood, on both our parts. How do I feel about this, really? It can't be self-hate that's causing my heart to leap at each bound of his legs. It can't be that I've *paid*—what can it be? Why am I happy? Do you call it love as he gathers me up and we push through the door and crash to the bed in a quick, shivery, clothes-on connection? Can you lust for the one you love so domestically?

And what, later, was that tender light in his eye?

In addition to writing his book, Roi has been fixing—with the help of a plumber and a carpenter—our new terrific attic. . . . A month to get heat and then more time for kitchen and john. So now it's all over but the cleaning, which is generously left to me, but I'm glad to be able to do something. . . .

Not that I'd been idle. Along with Roi's new chapter and the galley proofs of Frantz Fanon's *The Wretched of the Earth* to read for Grove Press, I'm carrying, next day as I board the bus to Newark, a paper bag of collard greens. Roi's grandmother, Anna Russ, who is keeping the children this morning, will show me how to grasp the bunch and make long slices, how to season the pot. The bus winds over the Jersey meadows, a generous vista in the clear spring air. There's clarity in separation too, I think. You begin to see what you miss. The fast words, for one thing, the tease. Roi and I have kept in touch through an answering service.

"Your hus*bean* says he'll call you at eight," the operator says, giggling.

By the time we reach Newark the greens are leaking onto the manuscripts. I hail a cab, and when the driver (white) frowns into the mirror, I calmly give him the address again. I'm used to all that. . . .

And here's a tiny girl on the porch—at nearly three she's so *important*. She says, leading me inside, "What did you bring?" I tumble my packages onto the table, and the bag breaks over two enormous oranges, bigger than softballs and round as globes. And it's then I notice Lisa, bouncing in her canvas chair, reaching out—and trying to *talk* to me! All these *words* are coming out of her mouth! How is this possible? She's become a *person*—overnight!

And then, suddenly, I remember William Phillips saying: "Don't have children. It doesn't work out."

Work out? He was anti-American, I think. These marvelous children. I fall on my knees in front of them.

"And what can I tell you about?"

This after everyone else was asleep, to Helene. The recent Happenings—precursors to Performance—didn't seem to compel me. Roi's book—newly titled *Blues People*—was going to be very good. His latest affair, with the ex-wife of the California poet

. . . didn't last long. Then he was sorry again. Poor Roi, he should never be a cocksman because he's directly out of the Baptist tradition and suffers more guilt and shame than anyone I know. As he did last spring and as I suppose he'll do again. . . . So I figure, being myself near to twenty-eight years old, and getting wiser every year

let him.

The person who wrote this? Who gave those last two words their own paragraph? I recognize her, a little. To be always chasing him only meant less time for her, and of the two, she was the more elusive.

He gave me a new name that year—H. Cohen-Jones—and surprised me with it on the last *Yugen* masthead. I liked it—it was funny to have the least aristocratic hyphenated name in America, although the up-front initial, H, somehow left out the woman whose mouth I was trying to open, this one:

Tomorrow we'll pack up and end this separation. Roi is to come and fetch us out of exile, up over and cross the river Jordan, to things to be done, new habits, new house, new work, we even—yeah, momma—have a new bed.

17

Periodically, depending on wind shift, Cooper Square filled with a foul smell from the Hartz Mountain Bird Food factory at number 26. The first time this attacked us I opened a window to find out the source and found myself looking down on our first-floor neighbor, Marzette Watts, who had just moved in. Especially seen from above, Marzette was a sight in those days, as he had stopped combing his hair. The short, twisted style he wore, though not uncommon now, hadn't been seen here since slavery, and in 1962 seemed improbable on this tall, dark, affable guy from Alabama, standing in front of you in a paint-spattered T-shirt, smoking a pipe of English tobacco. His friends shook their own shorn heads over him; in the street, passersby gawked. Black people say what goes around comes around, but only Marzette had completed the curve.

Like all artists living in formerly commercial spaces (27 had been a rooming house), Marzette spent some months on de- and reconstruction. His first ambition was to paint, so he took down all the many interior walls on his floor and made a loft, but then the outraged husband of one of his girlfriends smashed the glass in our real front door, broke into Marzette's, and slashed all his paintings. Soon after, he switched to music. Recording equipment was lugged upstairs, a soundproof ceiling installed, and down at the street the real door yielded to one of steel. Marzette settled down for a while with Ia, a beautiful slip of a red-haired Swede, who crocheted unusual, intricately patterned sweaters. The two of them became fond of Kellie and Lisa, for whom they often baby-sat, and who inspired, I guess, their own son, Dayoud.

For a time, when we were first on Cooper Square, the middle floor housed the Ezra Lasley Acting School. Ezra's students emoted—pleaded, raved, died—just below my kitchen, where, among the pots and pans, the posters for all the latest events, the sacred cowbells Allen and Peter had sent from India, and the curtains made from the last scraps of the Twentieth Street print bedspread, I hung a board Roi had painted with some Chinese characters. Every Day Is a Good Day, it said, and I hoped to remain convinced.

Mrs. Archie Shepp and I have just met in the A & P. We'd been quickly introduced once before, and I hadn't got her name right. "*Gaaath!*" she shouts with a Boston broad *a*. We're standing and grinning at each other, as if in a mirror at a good day's work. There, in her grocery cart, among the Cheerios and teething biscuits, are two boys about the same ages as my girls, also variously toned and equally pretty. Garth Shepp herself is beautiful, half-Jewish, half-Spanish, with lively eyes and jet black hair. She and Archie met at

Goddard College, came to New York, and are living on Sixth Street in two small rooms. He teaches homebound children when he isn't writing plays or composing or playing piano or tenor saxophone: he's only twenty-six but when Archie blows, people listen. Like Roi, all he has to do is do it.

Garth does it too. Weekdays she minds two more babies as well as her own. At night she sews—her clothes and the children's, bedding, curtains, and sometimes piecework—sleeves and sleeves and sleeves and sleeves for a St. Marks Place designer. She likes dye, too, so she's thinking about learning batiking, but what she really wants is a loom. . . . "Of course there's no room. . . ." She shrugs, and we laugh. And it's understood between us, as we block the aisle of the market with our matching cargoes, that we have bought a piece of the same action, into which—to give Garth the image—we will, *somehow*, weave the separate threads of our own ambitions.

A job like this wants company. After Ezra Lasley, and an interim student couple, the Shepps filled up the middle floor of 27 Cooper Square. Then, besides all the visiting poets and painters, the messages left, the overnight guests, the friends who depended on what they knew was the ongoing life here—"Fee Dawson and his wife, Barbara, called to ask if $45 was too much to pay for a refrigerator," I wrote Helene, "and would I please phone them at 7:15 A.M., if possible, as their alarm was broken and they had to *get to work the next day, early*"—besides all this was a new black music up close, from large, formal rehearsals to late-night improvisations, to what I loved and appreciated most: a solo from Archie's baby grand, the quiet, thoughtful chords of a slow morning blues. Sometimes, on my way up or down, I'd just sit on the stairs outside his studio door and listen.

After Ia left for Sweden, Marzette Watts took up with two sisters, Ann and Louise Holcomb, with whom he lived harmoniously while shocking the neighbors. None of us had doorbells—visitors called ahead or shouted up to the windows. Marzette's good friend, the trumpeter Don Cherry, would announce his arrival by playing a wooden flute, so clear it broke through the traffic noise. The acoustics of Cooper Square augmented every music: if it was warm weather when Archie's groups played, they'd open his studio windows and let the sound ricochet off the factories and repeat a millisecond later on the tenement wall on Fifth Street. The Five Spot was also only a stone's throw away. Roi was always hanging out the window. The casual proximity to his life of his chosen frame of reference, the source of so many images, made him deeply happy. And increasingly the racial balance in our house shifted, as a black avant-garde—writers, musicians, painters, dancers—became part of the new East Village, just coming into that name. The "Village East" gallery on St. Marks Place opened in January 1962, and though many painters—including Willem DeKooning, Larry Rivers, and Alfred Leslie—had long lived in the area, it wasn't until this year that a newspaper picture of Jim Dine was captioned "a well-known East Village artist." The real estate broker D. D. Stein offered his twenty-five-dollar bath-tub-in-kitchen apartments on Avenue B with the slogan "Join the Smart Trend," and the café Les Deux Mégots on Seventh Street advertised "Come East Young Man." Many of the people who eventually found their way to the neighborhood came to our house for parties, or to watch the "Fight of the Week," or simply to share a quart of Roi's favorite ale. We lined up the empties—for broke insurance—like a row of green sentinels on the stairs to the roof. There was always someone home when my new old clothes dryer blew the fuses, and the residential population itself increased. The Shepps produced two more children, Marzette and the Holcombs had four; like ours they grew sturdy legs to manage the stairs, and in the evenings, when their mothers let them, they commandeered the hall: Kellie, Lisa, Pavel, Accra, Bambu Ia, Dja'maa, Eli, LeDoux, Nicodemus, and Dasse—daredevils all on the old solid smooth brown banisters.

To run away from home I could run around the corner, to the second house on Fifth Street, where my friend Dorothy White lived in a basement store next to the boiler. Her husband, William, was a painter who'd been in the Air Force with Roi, and the first time I saw her—on Twentieth Street in 1959—she had a hairstyle not yet called a "natural" and a decade from being called an Afro. It fitted her face just right, like a soft round hat: what you see is what you got. We got along from the start—each with her own kind of disregard for appearances.

Many aspects of *like*ness attracted Dorothy and me—we saw ourselves in each other and approved. She admired my self-sufficiency, which reminded her, she said, of her own people. What I liked about her was her self-confidence, the self-esteem that had freed her to act on her feelings: you could be black or white but you'd better be good. She had fast feet, too, and a hearty laugh. One day I gave her a dress I'd made that no longer fit me, cut from a whole Indian cotton spread, tucked and retucked at the shoulders, pale yellow with red designs like flowers or eyes. I'd never seen anyone else in a dress I'd designed for myself. Dorothy wore it to a party that night, and watching her dance I felt her freedom to move as if it were my own, as if my intention had also been passed along. Dorothy shared too, and helped. She didn't have a child then, and sometimes she'd borrow mine; for them, hers was a known hand and lap: *Aunt* Dorothy, who took them to play in Brooklyn.

If contemporary black art, as defined by our husbands, had brought us together, a world of contemporary black women came to me in Dorothy's company. Some were the wives of painters and musicians, many had children, most had subverted ambitions; and given the prevailing racism and sexism, all of them were in for a hard time.

Dorothy's interest was art. Raised in Washington, D.C., one of ten children, with privacy scarce she hid under the porch. At ten she began her career, slipping into a whites-only museum. "But what brought you out from under the porch?" I asked. We were talking on the phone, and in the silence, as she thought about this, I imagined her slightly pursed lips, her frown, her round head thrown back. "A basket I made," she said finally. "I wove a basket in a summer playground program."

I said, "That was *my* basket you made."

She laughed, and said, "Is that right?"

More than to try her hand, it was an eye Dorothy was after. But she'd been self-supporting since her seventeenth year, and like most black women she saw no liberation in economic self-determination—she simply expected to have to earn a living for the rest of her life. As white women have since discovered, this has its effects. Mary McCarthy, in her *Memories of a Catholic Girlhood*, reminds us that there's much you can't learn later. Nevertheless you try. Days, Dorothy did market research, supporting herself and most of the time her husband. Evenings you'd find her with a book in front of her face, at home in their room behind his studio.

William White—always called White—was a tall, handsome, charming man who loved our baby and would fling her into the air, crying: "Lisa *Buns!*" After the Air Force he'd gone to Howard where he won prizes; one of his paintings hung in the Governor's Palace in Nigeria. He had a developing vision, you could see, a chaos of brush strokes coming out of the abstract. But the drug wolf had him hard by the throat, and shook him till he died. Dorothy did what she wanted eventually: had a daughter she called Zora, collected paintings, curated art shows. Never afraid to look come-what-may in the eye, she's my ace to this day.

Around another corner from us, past two bodegas and the gay 82 Club and little round Mr. Shnelwert's Hardware, was the building on Second Avenue where Basil and Martha King lived, which boasted the neighborhood's smallest and most out-of-service elevator. Every time I passed I sneered at Max, the owner, who'd refused me an apartment, and tried to make him into every Jew who'd shunned me. He didn't appear to notice.

Among the Poles and Ukrainians, Italians and Puerto Ricans, quite a few Jews still lived in the area, and paraded Second Avenue on Yom Kippur. The ghosts of Yiddish culture scowled behind the eyes of the waiters in Ratner's. I used to watch them with a detached fascination. Although I couldn't cease to think of myself as a Jew—a Semite really— I no longer felt Jewish, or sentimental about it. Something had broken. Basil had a studio across the street from Max's building, over the Anderson, once a Yiddish theater. With his kinky hair flattened back, and his face thrust out earnestly, he could have been one of the actors who played there. He'd come from London to the United States with his parents after World War II, left home for Black Mountain and became a painter with literary interests, contributing a good share of the covers for *Yugen* and Totem; later he was an editor of *Mulch*, an influential little magazine of the sixties. A much more domestic man than Roi but still an enfant terrible, grinding his cigarette into the floor and don't tell him not to. By 1962 Basil and Roi had been friends for five years. They were similar in stature. Neither could outdrink the other. They tried, of course. They would go from the Cedar to Dillons and on, sometimes joined by Gil Sorrentino, who was working for Grove Press on University Place and living in the neighborhood with his new wife, Vicky.

One evening the three of them ended up on Seventh Street in McSorley's, the bar that excluded women then. The habitués of McSorley's, many of them off-duty cops, would have liked to expand its exclusionary policies. Quietly at first, and then with more provocation, some of them began to insult Roi. Maybe they didn't expect a response, or understand that even if Gil and Basil were too drunk to stand they would have defended Roi's right to be anywhere. It was ten against three but they took it to the street, and when the on-duty cops finally arrived, Roi was down on the sidewalk being kicked.

At home, working, I knew none of this. About eleven I heard our garbage can being bumped up the stairs. Expecting Roi I opened the door to Basil. "Now it's *o-kay*," he said to my startled face.

But it didn't look okay. What he didn't know was that his face was beet red and swollen and his hair sprung up like Marzette's. And then he stood aside to reveal, below the garbage can on the nearly vertical stairs, Roi, looking sideways at me through a huge, purplish black shiner. Stumbling inside they careened through the narrow hall to the kitchen. "They each ate one shrimp," I wrote Helene, "and then fell asleep with their heads on their arms at opposite ends of the table."

"Home are the heroes, home from the wars." That a war had begun was something we knew and accepted, though it was still confined to the South and in the North only an "issue." "The Negro is on the march," reported the *Times*. But in which direction? That year a newly significant Muslim preacher named Malcolm X debated the labor leader Bayard Rustin about separation—not segregation—versus integration. In the downtown avant-garde it seemed to me then that all of us were going the same way, the only way that made sense. Certainly it was the only way I could ever accept. And looking at the twin bruised heads of Roi and Basil, I never thought that either one would ever be at war with the other.

18

St. Marks Place, in the early sixties, was a sleepy little city street with the shops of some young designers between the Ukrainian bar and the Domska Polska Nationalna. Most of these entrepreneurs were women, black and white, among them Khadeja, Jackie Lewis of Grand Hotel, Kristina Gorby (for whom Garth Shepp sewed sleeves), and Mary Rattray, who made jewelry at the Queen of Diamonds. Mary was assisted by her husband, the painter Howard Kanovitz, and for a time by Basil's wife, Martha King. The store was two steps down from the street, and sometimes as I approached I'd see Martha bent over a necklace she was stringing, her hair falling toward her face and the frown lines above her turned-up nose. And I'd feel—especially when pushing a carriage full of children—a flash of envy for her repose, that state Ron Loewinsohn caught:

> *The stillness of the poem*
> *a moment full of silence &*
> *portent, like*
> *the sudden halt of great machines.*

Other times, left simply to mind the store, Martha would be leaning idly against a counter, her eyes almost out of reach behind the prism of her thick glasses, as if she'd departed the beads and stones for another attraction. She'd met Basil at Black Mountain and from there her life had shifted to the not-quite-expected, raw at the edges; as a typical artist's wife most of her will toward self-expression went straight to resourcefulness. "I'm an occasional poet," she told her first publisher some years later. He disagreed. "You're a poet," he said, "who writes occasionally."

In 1962, pregnant with her first child, Martha turned to me for help as I'd turned to Rena. I told her all my stories. Anonymity, for instance, prized by artists, disappeared in the hospital clinic. At the time of Lisa's birth the social worker asked me, "Who's working, now, while you're here?" "No one," I answered. He didn't bother to hide his horror. As though dropped from the moon, you learned to stumble through, but no *decent* woman opened her legs to a man who couldn't support her. Therefore your pride, as you struggled home, was still located in *him*: he was right and you believed. "Bad Girls Get Lumps of Coal," read Mary Rattray's Christmas ad, "Good Girls Get Necklaces and Earrings from the Queen of Diamonds."

Because babies kept in a workplace couldn't be insured, Martha had to leave the Queen of Diamonds after her daughter, Mallory, was born, and instead went out evenings to work as a typist, but then eight months later she was pregnant again, surprised and a little ashamed. Like Joyce,

Martha had a strong proper streak—atop her improper bottom—and in all our discussions she'd never understood why I hated my diaphragm. Now she admitted that it wasn't made for a tired woman whose life might include a job, a nursing baby, an unpredictable husband, and more often than not—in Martha's case—a broken elevator and eight flights of stairs.

I complained to an expensive gynecologist: besides the diaphragm, and condoms that broke, wasn't there something? The doctor's advice was surreal: taking my hand she said, "You know, dear, you ought to get over being afraid of your husband."

It was Martha, later to write not only poems and stories but articles about medicine, who found the IUD experiment—after the birth of my namesake, Hetty, her second baby in seventeen months.

She called me, all excited and recruiting. "Our worries are over," she said. "They just put it in and leave it there."

"And it works?" I said.

"*They say* it works," she said.

"They say it works," I wrote Helene, after I'd submitted to the preliminary exam. "And if it does I'm going to write all over the mirrors in Ortho vaginal cream and maybe the walls. . . ."

As far as the city knew, 27 Cooper Square was a vacant, cold-water rooming house. "Loft living," considered a fire hazard, was illegal. Artists hid their beds and kitchens—even built false walls—while landlords turned their heads and held out their hands. Your money was good until the Fire Department caught you in your pajamas. Basil and Martha had been evicted from a loft. Joyce and Jim Johnson were playing cat and mouse with inspectors.

Facing us across the square was another illegally occupied four-story building, with a nice symmetry to its windows and a kind of sturdy authority, although it seemed much lower than ours because it was up against a factory three times its height. The playwright Aishah Rahman lived there, with a poet named Bobb Hamilton, who had two children he was raising, or rather Aishah was, a perfect example of Anna Freud's reminder that the parent is the one who does the parenting. After the hardest work was over and the children well settled in school, Aishah herself left for school, in Washington, where she cleaned a dozen hotel rooms a day to pay her tuition at Howard. Then she traveled on, to a master's degree, a child of her own, and various productions to her credit, and it took me a few more years to catch up with her again. At which point she let me have what she'd been saving. "You asked me then how I could leave," she said. "You didn't see where I *was*." And she made her arms into Cooper Square. "You didn't see how *down* I was"—she pointed to her building—"because you were always up *there!*"

This was true for most of us. Joyce never mentioned she'd stopped writing. Martha couldn't say what she wanted. I kept my own "occasional poems" to myself, looking *at*, but not behind, Aishah's windows. In retrospect there's some terrible shame—how *could* we?

But I am only stumbling toward my own why here.

Roi had begun to write drama. In the spring of 1962 a student director at the Actors Studio staged his play *The Toilet*, which broached the forbidden subject of interracial homosexual attraction. We went to Lee Strasberg's master class, where the tone was serious and respectful, and the work very well received; Strasberg, the Studio director, urged Roi to try to raise money for an Off Broadway run.

Afterward, on the winged feet of congratulation, we set out to walk all the way crosstown from the far west forties to the East River, headed for a cocktail party at the UN. It was late in the afternoon, and I'd become so matter-of-fact about race that I was jolted by the shocked expressions, the staring of suburban commuters. Midway, at Fifth Avenue, I glanced at Roi to see how he was, whether he had that tight look on his face. But he seemed fine, and perfectly self-satisfied, and why not? He'd said in *The Toilet* what he wanted to say, and now he'd been applauded for it. He had also, magically, procured for the occasion a store-bought dress—my first in five years. A thank-you? A salary? I thought of him that morning, making faces for the laughing children. "Hey, The King," I said fondly, and took his hand. But he just grinned and ducked his head and then let go of my hand when the light changed, and away we charged across the street, him with his runner's stride and me with my short legs determinedly keeping pace.

At the party, hosted by the Cuban delegation, I had a lot of fun on four martinis, which sent me right on the nod over dinner. "How unsophisticated," I wrote Helene, and oh, the amusement on Roi's face when I opened an eye and spied my untouched plate. He was a famous sleeper—he'd nod off anywhere—and he loved to see it happen to someone else!

In the forties you bought a record after you'd played it in the store. From the fifties on, after records came sealed in plastic, liner notes had to be more convincing. The increasingly urbane jazz audience liked to be told what it was buying. Roi was able to get this work, which never paid very much. He went to lunch one day with a man from United Artists. Talking terms, he said he wanted to be paid on receipt of the material (instead of the usual lengthy delay). "Oh, do you need *money?*" said the surprised executive. Said Roi, shocked: "Man, I *always* need money."

"So the cat hands him a twenty," I wrote Helene, "just for love, you know, and good business connections." We spent it immediately, on a sitter, a movie, and drinks at the Cedar. "The presumption!" Roi kept shouting. "The fucking presumption!"

But the next day he wrote a short essay—I called it "a lovely pageful of words"—about Billie Holiday. It began: "Nothing was more perfect than what she was. Nor more willing to fail." I think Roi was game to see where a woman could go, but like Billie she had to go herself, and as for *my*self, he didn't see *him*self in the way. Still his lovely pageful of words hit home. "A voice that grew from a singer's instrument to a woman's," he wrote. "Sometimes you are afraid to listen to this lady."

In the nineteenth century, Emerson called on women to write "the meaning of a household life." I found that goal elusive a century later.

I didn't *mind* my household life, I just couldn't do a damn thing with it. How did it translate to words, this holding pattern of call and response, clean and dirty, sick, well, asleep, awake. Its only allure was need, and need was just a swamp behind the hothouse of desire—how could you want what you had to have? I could only record my time, and send it on:

> Took myself and children over to Jersey, to and fro on the bus, the fro trip complicated by Lisa throwing up all over. . . . Got them to bed by 9:30, cleaned up mess made by Roi alone in the house all day, made twelve bucks [three hours] checking a Random House book by old *Partisan Review* standby Sidney Hook. And now, having come up from under the vomit and *Education for Modern Man*, in from the chilly kitchen to this warm papery room,

I feel *good*. Nothing exists, even the Bowery's shut out. . . .

But where to go, after all that? Certainly not to writing that makes any further demands on feeling, which requires strength as well as time. Marina Tsvetayeva complained, in her journal, "I am always in the presence of others, from 7 in the morning till 10 at night, and by 10 at night I am so exhausted—what feeling can there be? No, I simply sit down to mend and darn. . . ."

Like mending and darning, observation is just a release, a way to get something done. You can talk politics:

> Just watching [on TV] Mr. Kennedy and his boys, and their countersubversion in South America. "What we have to fear [said the newscaster] are the *students* [italics mine] who have been trained in Havana as subversives!"

Social history:

> The Cedar finally closed, with Joel Oppenheimer the last paying customer. The building and those adjacent for half a block are to be torn down to make way for a monstrous apartment house and those who think the Village is so charming. Soon the Village will be all monstrous apartment houses with no charm for the suckers who come to find it.

Comparative economics:

> Roi just called from midtown, gave me 7,000 guesses to guess who he was with. I made it in two but then sort of caved in when I heard that Edw. Albee earns, per week from *Virginia Woolf*, twice as much as we do in a year!

The progress of children:

Kellie so jumpy and merry, her round little
cheeks. The other day she said: "I love you, Mommy,
because you're so *intelligent*."

Beautiful Lisa, thigh deep in autumn leaves,
says her name is Zi-SAH! And with her arms flung
around my neck, a whispered confession: "I *love*
my Daddy."

And then, inevitably:

Now our nightly Noise from the Bedroom
Program. I bring water to K, who coughs as though
she were choking to death which wakes L, who
refuses water or any small comfort and who will
only quiet when taken into my bed. Every five
minutes, sometimes all night. . . . That last took half
an hour and four trips down the hall. And another
since I wrote that. And since it's 2:30 I'll give
up. . . .

My cigarette's in an ash tray with an irremovable
decal, a picture of a spinning wheel and Mary
Washington College. . . . I've tried steel wool but it
won't come off. . . .

Like Tsvetayeva's notebook, which kept her "above the
surface of the waters," the letters I sent to Helene kept me
from sinking:

So dahling this is life in the cosmopole après
la saison. I'm now going to board my little boat and
speed down to meet a young gallant who follows
me everywhere though I am utterly chaste. But
then I dilate my nostrils, which sends him into a
spasm of desire, to alleviate which he descends on
the Guggenheim Foundation, and brings me on
the end of his sword a $5,000 fellowship, which he

places on my left breast, murmuring "I'll get Ford for the right." Then he disappears in the night.

If I sleep long enough, will he bring a Rockefeller for the snatch? I think this typewriter cheers me. Sometimes it's the little things, chérie, that are so important. Tu sais? Tu connais? Vraiment, les choses petites de la vie bohème. Ah, me. I promise to write more, better, sooner, oftener.

Kay Boyle, writing of memory's "dreamy, evasive eyes," says there's no way even the honest among us can be trusted. There were days, though, that I seemed to have swallowed whole, as if I knew there'd be more to say eventually. But it was fifteen years, and I was another person when that happened:

On the bus
from Newark to New York
the baby pukes
into the fox collar
of her only coat

She wipes the collar
and the baby's soft face
then takes her toddler
by the hand
and heads for the subway

where the toddler
sleeps
at her knee
and she
    herself
stares
out the window
over the head
of the sleeping baby
She is twenty-seven
and very tired

     Let me always
support her
     Having been her
befriend her

19

To push out the poor it barely acknowledged, the city had condemned certain "slum areas." One began just south of us, across Fifth Street, and included the first Five Spot, which went down, poof!—and with it some of our history. Clearing out Tompkins Square Park was also part of the plan: its tall trees would have gone for a ball field if the community hadn't protested.

Cooper Square was the western border of the new East Village, Tompkins Square its center. By 1962, like everyone else I knew, I had crossed and recrossed the park at all hours, encountered all my old loves there. Sometimes, when I wasn't working, I sat with other young mothers at a sandbox near Avenue B. We kept to ourselves but we were a presence, a neighborhood in the original sense of the word—not a place but the people who live there. Around us all the Ukrainian, Polish, Jewish, and Italian *babushkas* gathered, and their querulous men who'd glare at us from the benches. But we were good for business—we bought their vegetables, their brightly flowered scarves and irregular socks. I liked the quick park exchange, that moment where old and new took equal offense and I could measure our cultural strengths, our freedom against their overdressed babies and angry toddlers, all those longing teenage eyes lured by our sexy lives. Right in the middle of the old, the park was full of future flashes.

In a neighborhood as it's commonly defined, you often catch certain people in certain places. The pianist Cecil Taylor invariably came walking toward me up Sixth Street, small and tight as a hard brown nut, but the gentlest of acquaintances, always *glad* to see me, just like Albert Ayler, whom I'd meet on St. Marks Place, and from whose courtly manner and smile you'd never suspect the screams he coaxed from his saxophone. Musicians, like women, hauled and carried and were the poorest, and since there were very few clubs they often played in lofts that were not yet seas of urethane but scarred, splintering spaces with cracked windows and rudimentary plumbing. (At one such place I sat very close to Cecil, watching him roll the piano keys into sounds I'd tried as a kid but never imagined could be extended, and coalesced. It was like bathing in music. Cecil rocked and so did I and so did the floor.) I'd always pass the drummer Sonny Murray on Fourth Street, in his one jacket, struggling with his trap set and no money for a taxi. Another Sonny— the saxophonist Sonny Rollins—lived below Houston near Clinton Street, where one day Roi and I ran into him, a standout among all the *yarmulkas*. He'd been a cowboy on his album *Way Out West*, and now, as if again to insist on his history, there he was in a Mohawk haircut. (No one copied him; for years he stood alone, on the long, complicated cultural road between the real thing and the punk imitation.)

On the afternoon of Lisa's first birthday it's ninety-six degrees and about the same humidity. Since our celebrations are large so is the cake, balanced on the hood of an unfamiliar carriage I'm pushing along First Avenue, on loan to us because our fourth carriage has just been stolen from the downstairs hallway. This is what you have to expect, living on the Bowery, but I didn't expect any carriage to be unequal to my load, and suddenly—watch out!—we're tipping! Lisa, half asleep, cries out, setting off Kellie, astraddle her sister's legs and loyally clutching the string of the cake box. It's a scene I've repeated, and repeated. Writing about it later, I'll call myself "Old Mother Jones in clothes that were stuck to her old mother bones."

In a gloom of self-pity—spiced with self-loathing—I get a good grip and keep plodding. But then around the corner comes Ornette Coleman, whom I always meet on First Avenue. In his hand is the plastic horn with which he has taken New York by storm and which will lead him to international acclaim and the distinction of being imitated, everywhere, on all kinds of instruments, and music—even what is not called jazz—will incorporate his sound. But now, on August 15, 1962, like me he's under the burning sun—Texas-born, left-handed Ornette, a medium-size man whose eyes crinkle up when he smiles. Which he does, saying, "Hey, man." And I'm redeemed. Despite my doubts—despite this different life—I'm a man among men.

M y mother, who never met any of these people, considered me her duty, kept up with me in secret, and twice a year would climb our stairs in a pleasant, martyred sweat. She happened to visit that summer when Roi, inspired by the children's colored chalk, had written some libelous notes about current public figures (Allen D—— is queer, Norman M—— is colored, Allen T—— and Lionel T—— are in love). Libelous but hilarious, I thought, and just where I liked them: all over the walls of the bathroom. My mother thought this "absolutely juvenile."

Soon I had a letter from her, in which she said, among other things, that I would suffer and pay every minute of my life—those her exact words—for the kind of life I had chosen. And what really ticked her off was that I seemed happy. Could it be, she wondered, that I was "really a good actress"? To Helene, spoofing the poet Michael McClure, I wrote, "I AM NOT SHIT FUCK DAMN HELL I AM HAPPY."

"Or maybe just happy," I added, hedging.

The next day, again pushing my loaded buggy, I passed a construction worker who said, peering over his hammer, "Those are sure some pretty babies, but they sure don't look like you."

"And they sure don't look like *you*," I replied smoothly.

But the remark set me up, and, with due respect to my mother's intuition, I then came face to face, buggy to buggy, with Diane Di Prima, who had her new baby out, which didn't look like *her*, either. Conceived—without Roi's knowledge or consent, so he later said—during our separation the previous year (he'd subsequently stopped seeing Diane).

I admired Diane—why not? She wrote. Her self-directed life included a lot of good work. But her plans for Roi were far from his own. He'd written—in the story "Going Down Slow"—that when he was with her he always knew where his pants were. Which hardly mattered now, since by the time he put them on he'd risked his history. I looked at the dark brow, the familiar features of Diane's baby. It was hard—*hard*—for me to admit she existed.

Roi wouldn't, not at first. When I got home and told

him what I'd seen, he said, "They all look alike." We were standing in the kitchen in front of the Every Day Is a Good Day sign. My horror at what he'd said must have shown because without another word he hurried guiltily from the room.

Diane then moved two doors away, on Cooper Square, with her little girl and the baby, Dominique. Eventually she married, moved to California, married again, and had several more children. But while I had to see her I never could find the proper response. Roi himself made no response to the child. "We had a few bad days," I wrote Helene, "with him sneaking about the house trying to avoid my scathing looks." The situation was tough to ignore. "If I send you a D doll, will you stick pins in it?" Actually I stayed angry a long time. But I also was, as I wrote, "never one to commit infanticide." And anger has its own kind of string. Unless you let it go, it ties you down.

Roi's sister, Elaine (later Kimako Baraka), had been leading a show-biz life in Europe, and last we'd heard she was dancing in the Richard Burton–Elizabeth Taylor remake of *Cleopatra*. One day in the summer of 1962 she appeared out of the blue under our windows, with an enormous leather shoulder bag, a portfolio, and—as I discovered after she'd come upstairs—a mouthful of Italian accent.

Five years had added to the wiry girl I'd gotten to know on a Sunday afternoon in 1957, in her family's kitchen, while she pressed her hair with a curling iron, the kind you heat on the stove. The same hot threat, I told her, that my mother had used on me. We always joked about that, and other dilemmas of race and sex; Elaine had her brother's dry humor, though lacking his sharp, cruel edge. She was just finishing teachers college then, with Roi urging her out of the middle class ("Hymn for Lanie Poo"); he wanted her more than she was, or different, like the black women making their way in downtown Manhattan. But Elaine wanted her own life. She left for Europe when Kellie was doll-sized.

And now here she was, transfigured! A fashion plate in shades and a bright yellow skirt. But if I was amazed at her, she herself was astounded by her nieces. "They walk!" she marveled. "They talk!" Roi wasn't home so I took her to the park, sat her down on a bench, and pumped her for tales of European high life. She had those, including the Burton-Taylor dressing-room love affair, and plenty more about being broke, and black, and traveling.

From then on Elaine and I kept in touch, spent holidays together; sometimes she'd borrow her mother's car and haul us all to Newark. She continued to dance, on Broadway, in *Sweet Charity* and other shows; she produced, directed, organized, taught first grade to college. Later she did follow Roi, took advantage of the name he had made, but she never had an easy time, and in her forties she died. The obituaries focused on her brother, although among her many credits was the organization of probably the first-ever block party. Like all the other people we knew who left us before they should have, I had counted her a presence to be reckoned with, not an absence to be felt. I miss her at Christmas. I carry her pocketbook. I remember how she dressed in layers—long before the fashion—and would strip just to impress us! I like to remember her best that day she met her tiny new relatives, when she was fresh from her glamorous expatriate experience, a strong young woman in her twenty-sixth summer, sitting in Tompkins Square Park with her brown legs stretched out, her short skirt riding up, and all her sophisticated angles soft with delight.

Among those sharing our bench that day were women who couldn't have told you that in twenty-five years they'd be featured in *The New York Times*. The dancer Sally Gross had been in Robert Frank's movie *Pull My Daisy*, but since then she'd married a musician, had two children, and was teaching school. Within a few years her husband would be dead. Her deep-set eyes held a steady, stubborn focus, as if somewhere she were on fire. Vertamae Grosvenor, with whom I'd acted at the Judson, had just had her second daughter. Like Roi's involvement with jazz, her interest in food was a road to reclaim black culture, a term not yet invented when she stood at the stove with a spatula in her hand and a newborn on her shoulder, explaining to me that salt in the pan would keep pork chops from sticking.

Also at our sandbox were women who couldn't imagine their lives legitimized—unmarried mothers, mothers of interracial children like Verta's and mine. We thought of ourselves as free because of the risks we'd taken, though we weren't free at all. In any case what had emancipation to do with endurance? "No one ever told me," cried Verta, "that I was going to be a mother *forever*."

The books I worked on were all by men or about them, with women seen from their viewpoint. But the groups of women I knew—in classes, clinics, at the park—were not as men described them. And so many of them were *needy*. As soon as Kellie turned three I put her in a Department of Welfare day care center. The fee was two dollars a week, and proof required that although married you still had to work. But it was a good place, in the large, airy rooms of a local settlement house, and soon—embarrassed and defensive, as if I'd joined the dreaded system—I wrote Helene: "What will you say when I tell you I'm on the *school board*!"

Helene herself led an unexpected life in unexpected places. Without the support of the park bench, the isolation was profound. "Sometimes," she wrote, "I hear 'Pocatello, Idaho' on the radio and I still can't believe that I'm in it!"

Neither one of the Dorns liked city life: Ed found its

rush and unconcern offensive, and Helene was scared: "I can kill the black widows in the corners of the outhouse, watch the scorpions crawl, walk through sage and rocks where rattlesnakes abound. . . . But the subway!" Nevertheless, at the end of the summer of 1962, the summer that Martin Luther King was jailed from a segregated courtroom in Albany, Georgia, the summer that Jamaica and Trinidad and Tobago finally became free nations, the summer that Marilyn Monroe died and the Five Spot moved three blocks north, the Dorns decided to risk New York: "O well— scorpions, subways," wrote Helene. "Take me a week to get to Coney Island any other way, wouldn't it?"

For a while we had a little Black Mountain, with its absorptions and passionate attractions. First Ed and Helene arrived with two of their children, and then the following week, along with the Dorns, we made room for Charles and Betty Olson.

Years later, struggling to find the person I was in the one I'd become, I wrote a story about myself and Charles, to whom I felt deeply indebted. Here it is, *in memoriam.*

He was such a tall man, the famous older poet, that there were parts of the kitchen where he couldn't stand straight, so she sat him down at the far end where he appeared, sitting, like any normal man, eating his breakfast eggs. To her, a mother still in her twenties, he was a man of whom she might have been in awe. But she wasn't—either because he put her at ease, or because she was then more arrogant and self-assured than I remember. She was very small, and only came up to his waist. When they'd met, the previous evening, much was made of this difference.

Then a child came running in, the younger one, just learning to talk and seeming incredibly small in the perspective lent by the tall man. She bent, conscientiously, to the child, explaining something: a lesson about responsibility, teaching that word, is what I seem to remember.

The man ate, listening to her, though she wasn't aware of this as there were other people in and out, eating. It was after the child left that he complimented her: "I like the way you use language," he said.

She felt humble but warmed to him immediately, pleased that he liked what she hadn't yet proven, and no one had so quickly read her heart. His opinion of her gave her courage. She withheld nothing. They became friends, and it was the nature of the occasion that they should have, since the tall man and his wife, and another good man and his good wife, had come to spend a week—luckily that week because that week there was no money for food and it was terrific that these guests had arrived and could buy food for everyone. And they could admire themselves for feeding six adults and two children on chicken backs and carrots, for poetry and justice for all. She was having a great time. She cornered the older poet and pressed for his secrets: What is your wife to you, she demanded, then confided that she sometimes thought her husband didn't love her. But there he demurred, saying, no, I have seen the two of you, I have seen you, sleeping, together.

It was his gentle emphasis on the word, sleeping, that held her ear and therefore her imagination, and so holds me, now. It was the note only that she heard, there in the narrow hall, standing literally under his arm and him bending over, as she had bent to the child. I can see now what she couldn't have known then, though she wanted to believe him: he was so much older and wiser than she and she trusted him so. But she had only her young woman's point of view, and she was certain that a man—even he—couldn't know the whole of it. She nodded and leaned close, to let him know she'd understood his lesson—what one word, one tone, could mean. But she kept her face averted, hiding her refusal to accept his judgment, just that once.

Of the remaining events of this time, I recall a rowdy scene in an uptown subway station after a boring literary party, and he, though gray, not out of place among the enfants terribles. And her dancing with him while everyone laughed. Although they two were politely respecting the dance: it was the others who once again saw their disparity while they, the principals, had passed it by.

Later he wrote her some funny, friendly letters that were mostly about business, poems of his I think, which she kept for a long while and then sold to pay the rent. By that time he was dead. She minded selling the letters but didn't feel guilty. He would certainly have understood, she thought, living on chicken backs. Anyway she chose to keep not what the man wrote her from his desk, but what she felt he had truly given her, what occurred between them. And I am left with her choices.

20

In 1960 Marc Schleifer, an aspiring journalist hanging around our house on Twentieth Street, began—with guidance from the resident group—a magazine of comment and criticism called, after much debate, *Kulchur*. Financial backing came from Lita Hornick, a wealthy matron who later assumed the editorship, but the initial credit must go to Marc, although he stuck around for only one issue (and ended up a correspondent in the Middle East, renamed Suleiman Abdullah). In 1962, still Schleifer, he left for Cuba with the photographer Leroy McLucas, who was having a show there. Soon I had a letter from these travelers, oddly sent to me not at home but in care of Marian Zazeela, Marc's first wife. I guess they didn't want Roi to see it. "Dear Hettie," it read, "Tonight, talking it over, we discovered that we share you as Our Secret Love. Your Secret Lovers, Marc *y* McLucas." They must have been a sight to behold, six-foot Marc, the Jewish image of a *shagetz*, and skinny, hollow-cheeked black Mc-Lucas, wandering the streets of revolutionary Cuba, and laid up writing love letters in the Hotel Presidente. But I was happy at the thought of them there, and pleased that they'd thought about loving me, secretly, separately, and together, and it pleased me, too, that *Kulchur* had survived.

Frank O'Hara, Gil Sorrentino, and Roi were among others on its editorial board, and with their contributions the magazine was interesting and lively. But Lita Hornick's dining room was the first I'd seen with a buzzer under the table to summon the maid, and when I had dinner there I was the only person seated who really *was* a maid like the one who appeared. Still, Lita was short and had to grope for her buzzer, and then half rise to press it with the toe of her high-heeled shoe. She was fair and a little plump and her face flushed up each time. I settled down and drank my wine and reconciled myself. Lita was generous; all the downtown artists crowded her large Park Avenue apartment for parties. And to me she was kind.

Lita and her husband, Morton, once took Roi and me to an expensive restaurant. Roi, the only black person in the room, was his usual self-confident self. Like him I could usually hold my own, but that night I was terribly hungry and the food so good that I went on eating and eating until at a lull I looked up to find everyone finished, waiting patiently for me to stop. A bite of delicious fish with little green grapes was left but I couldn't go back to it; I felt starved and ashamed. Maybe I knew I had to eat while I could. "Someday," I wrote Helene with gloomy foresight, "I will probably be classed as 'charming but noncontributing,' and Lita will no longer take me to dinner."

Roi's essay "Tokenism: 300 Years for Five Cents" was first published in *Kulchur*, and the word has stayed in the language as he intended. A few weeks after publication Martin Luther King used it on the radio, and gave the essay and its author credit. I've always thought this just the right irony: the right word in the right place at the right time, published by the lady from Park Avenue.

The nonviolent civil disobedience of the early sixties did not lack scenes of dreadful violence: black people water-hosed and police-dogged by their lawful local governments, busloads of blacks-and-whites-together bloodied before being arrested. By the fall of 1962 there had been "nonviolent" demonstrations involving thousands of people in hundreds of cities in more than half the states. In October, President Kennedy called out federal troops to enroll one black man, James Meredith, in the University of Mississippi.

But the United States was still a Cold War imperial power, and the CIA was hard at work in the not-yet-called Third World; we kept pictures on our walls of Patrice Lumumba, the Congo's murdered young leader. October 1962 was also the month that President Kennedy quarantined Cuba, setting off a terrifying crisis over Soviet missiles there. For a moment it looked as if we'd have an atomic war with the Soviet Union and New York City would be a prime target. It didn't help that our sympathies lay with Fidel. "Hello out there where the bombs may not go (?)" I wrote Helene. "Can't say much because my hand is shaking."

About this time Roi appeared on a program at Town Hall, where he urged more and stronger protest against both local and federal governments. The applause was loud and lengthy. Gramma had come with us and at its height was just sitting there, across the aisle from me, hands folded in her lap. Roi had spoken with vehemence against her generation, calling them all Uncle Toms, and I was concerned about her reaction. I crouched beside her seat and asked if she were angry.

"Angry? Are you kidding?" she said, turning to me. There was a lot going on behind her eyes. It was only later that I remembered her father's store going up in flames, the blow to his head that ended his conscious life.

In the winter of 1963 Roi began teaching at the New School, and not surprisingly proved good at it, and popular with his students. In addition, his book *Blues People* was at last in page proof, he was editing a collection of stories for Eli and Ted Wilentz's Corinth Books, and he'd actually been paid for a poem—thirty-seven dollars, by *Evergreen Review*. His poetry and criticism had also appeared in the *Provincetown Review*, *Massachusetts Review*, the *Nation*, *Poetry*, and a dozen others, and his photo had been taken for the September special issue of *Ebony*. All this success became him. He was fun to be around. Sometimes he sang at the top of his lungs all the songs he knew strung together. To get through the slushy winter he bought huge, heavy boots that left marks like baby tanks all over the house. "Out of the way, you midgets!" he'd cry, stomping down the hall toward the children who would fling themselves at him in fits of giggles.

Recognition didn't equal money: "We're penniless again," I wrote Helene, "so it'll take a few days until I can spare the eight cents to mail this." With free-lance work too chancy, I pawned my portable typewriter and took a part-time job, at the Wilentzes' Eighth Street Bookshop, where I sorted bills and checks in a room I described as "dinky as *PR*, maybe dinkier, but much less depressing." A.B. Spellman was clerking in the shop then, and it was pleasant to work for Ted and Eli, who'd been so supportive. But after a week's labor, and child care, I had thirteen dollars. Still I couldn't make the trip uptown, like Joyce Johnson and Sara Blackburn did, like Roi himself had done for almost a year. "Insanity, inertia, and refusal to leave the kids too long" were the reasons I listed.

What's missing is critical: the way I now felt in whites-only groups. In a midtown office by himself, Roi could only be himself. In a similar situation, without him or the children, I felt misrepresented, minus a crucial dimension, and seeing race prejudice everywhere, shocking and painful. Other whites in black families speak of this; Diana Powell, who sometimes baby-sat for me, later married actor-director Douglas Turner Ward and is herself the mother of two black children. She calls it feeling "disguised in your own skin."

One evening that winter, still without my own typewriter, I pulled out of Roi's what appeared to be the very beginning of a play with three characters, abbreviated *Gra*, *Wal*, and *Eas*. "Hi Hel," I wrote, "this is Het." The following year, *Gra* (Grace)—although transmuted to a tall, blond WASP—would be taken for me. Nowhere in her character is this feeling that had so changed me. Of course to express it was up to me, not Roi. But I had pawned my typewriter. It was Hettie Cohen's portable. I never got it back—and really it was just too slow.

By the spring of that year the South was seething with demonstrators and "outside agitators"; there had been action in eight hundred American cities. Tear gas and cattle prods had been used, as well as dogs and water hoses strong enough to strip the bark from trees. The whole world had reporters in Birmingham, sometimes called Bombingham, Alabama, where Police Commissioner Bull Conner said, "Damn the law. Down here I am the law." It was no longer possible to ignore the war that for a century had been called "our Negro problem."

Roi's position was, "It's *your* Negro problem." But if the problem is yours, who are you? And what about me? Was it because I didn't—couldn't—describe my own position that *Gra*, the woman Roi was writing, came into being? Was I a stranger to him as I was to the whites I avoided?

On an otherwise fine, blossomy day in May, I found myself at the doctors station in the public ward of Bellevue Hospital. Beside me Roi was slumped in a wheelchair. Except for him, everything I could see was green—the doctor's scrub suit, the bedsteads, the old walls. But Roi was yellow ochre and his eyeballs looked shockingly like my Queen of Diamonds amber necklace. He'd been sick for two weeks and now they said it was hepatitis. Was it "dirty needle" or infectious? When questioned, he admitted to having shot heroin. "Why didn't you *stop* him?" the doctor demanded of me angrily.

Stop *him*? I knew he'd been getting high on occasion with White and Bob Thompson, but I also knew that Roi was too ambitious, and loved himself too much, to become an addict. "It's *his life*," I said snootily to the doctor, who turned away in disgust.

Deciding he was not infectious, they kept him in a fifty-bed ward full of old, neglected men, where he was surrounded, for two weeks, by flowers from his students, stacks of books and cards and letters, and an enormous basket of fruit from Lita Hornick. Then he came home for an hour, thin and hungry and horny, whispering, in our bedroom, before I shipped him off to rest in Newark, "I thought about you every day."

Maybe we shouldn't have entered that room. One afternoon the following week my legs buckled under me suddenly; I barely made it home from work and up the stairs. Despite the Bellevue doctor's assumption, Roi had infectious hepatitis, and now I had it too—a mild case, my eyes were only lemons. And so we switched around: I went to bed, the children went to Newark, and Roi, recovered some, came home to take care of me.

I lay abed like Camille, reading *Thought and Religion in*

Ancient Mexico while he went to the supermarket. My mother arrived to make chicken soup, bringing a check from my father, who'd refused to write my name on it! But he didn't like to think of me suffering, my mother reported soberly, having forgotten, I suppose, her prediction that I'd suffer the rest of my life. Both Roi and I wanted to send back the check. "I wish we didn't need it," he said. But we did. We were broke. Ted Wilentz got me workmen's compensation. A benefit night of poetry and music was held for us at the Living Theatre.

It was a hepatitis honeymoon. We hadn't been alone in four years. To make love in the daytime we usually had to hide from the sharp-eyed children. (One morning they ran in then out, whispering, "I *saw* them, I *saw* them!") Now it was sweet to be able to strip in the summer sunshine under the skylight. And how terrific to watch the whole thing happen, in ecstatic operation. "Oh look at us, look at us!" I cried.

The following year, in a bitter discussion about race, it turned out he'd thought I meant "Look at us, look at black and white." How sad that made me feel, when I'd only meant the gizmo, the one that practice makes perfect.

It's a bright fall noon but not where I am, nineteen floors above Sixth Avenue at Fifty-first Street, in a corridor that makes me think of death row. Suddenly I feel something wrong: it's my chewing gum. I reach for something to stick it to. In my bag there's only an unfinished note to Helene, about our first posthepatitis drinks at yesterday's publisher's lunch for Roi. *Blues People* came out in late September. Writing in the New York *Herald Tribune*, Nat Hentoff called it "a jazz masterpiece." Everyone's excited. There will be parties. . . .

But of course we're still broke, which is why I'm finally

here, at Time, Inc. I pass an open door. Far away is a snatch of the season I've just left. A wave of stubborn self-pity stops me. I want to be in my kitchen, with the roof door open. . . .

At the end of the corridor is an interviewer in a white shirt and blue suit, in which I hope he feels safe as he doesn't seem comfortable. I parry the questions about the children duly listed on my resume. What about illness, absenteeism? He asks me *why* I'm a working mother. I don't mention Roi's name; it's not on my resume.

While my proofreading test is being checked I pick up a copy of *Time* from several weeks before, showing thousands of people soaking their tired feet in the pool at the Washington Monument. It's four weeks since the March on Washington and Martin Luther King's "I Have a Dream" speech. Not everyone feels as patient as Dr. King. Our bathroom graffiti includes "Booker T. Washington in drag." Dreams, some people say, are no substitute for freedom *now*, voting rights, equal protection under the law. Eighteen days after the March, four black teenage girls were killed, in Birmingham, when dynamite was thrown into their Sunday-school classroom.

My test score is 92. I qualify, I'll be put on the list, but first I must work (free) for a couple of hours. Walking to the proofreader's office, I note something I'd never imagined, a hierarchy of light: women work in the dark heart of Time, while only men have windows onto the weather.

Mention is made that in last week's issue there was an error: E.E. for e.e. cummings. I remember the anguished face of William Phillips, when I'd missed a book ad in *Partisan Review* for Steven not Stephen Spender. I consider revealing this as an offer of comfort, because the readers—two young men and a woman—seem ashamed. I think of the many times I've been Mrs. Leroy instead of LeRoi, who is himself, at this precise moment, on the corner of St. Marks and Third, behind the new Five Spot's sun-warmed windows, having his picture taken by a *Time* photographer for a feature review of his book.

That night I wrote: "Did not get to see Mr. Luce. After five hours there, was ready for downtown you can be sure. Should I let them find out slowly, by accident, that we are the people they most fear?"

A month later Corinth published *The Moderns: An Anthology of New Writing in America*, with stories by Burroughs, Creeley, Kerouac, and John Rechy among others, edited and with an introduction by Roi, in whom the critics found a double whammy, an ace of the avant-garde who was—so surprisingly—black. A new Negro writer! was the general exclamation, as if that could only be seen as phenomenon, which caused the Joneses profound amusement. Roi had dedicated *Blues People* to his parents, "the first Negroes I ever met." "Gee," said Gramma. "And I was going to keep it from him."

Everyone else, it seemed, was out to discuss it: *The Nation, Saturday Review, Newsweek*—but mysteriously not *Time*, where I'd been offered a job but had to refuse as I was suddenly needed at home to answer the phone and keep out the world. In which new complications arose when President Kennedy was killed and the reputed assassin was connected to the Fair Play for Cuba Committee. Roi had given the New York chapter of that organization his name to use—he didn't actually work for them—and soon our phone broke, and I joked that it had rung itself out until one day he found some men on the roof, who'd scaled a three-story wall to repair, they said, the line. Said Joel, whenever he heard any extra sizzle and couldn't get through: "You bastards could at least take a message."

In January 1964, Roi's play *Dutchman* was showcased by the Playwrights Unit, established by Edward Albee and others and supported initially by those profits from *Virginia Woolf* that had so astonished me. In *Dutchman* an older white woman kills—on the subway—the young, middle-class black man she's been tormenting. But not, of course, before he speaks his mind. The audience at the Van Dam Theatre responded with a standing ovation. Cicely Tyson, then the only young black woman in a TV series, was behind us shouting "Author! Author!" Roi sat grinning into the darkness, hunched in his old tweed jacket.

Afterward, in the hubbub of handshake and congratulation, a woman came running up to me and seized me out of the crowd. "I knew it!" she shouted. "I knew you'd go somewhere!" She'd last seen me in 1951, when for a semester she taught acting at Mary Washington; now she worked with the Playwrights Unit. She was so happy and excited to find me that I didn't have the heart to remind her: it wasn't *my* play they'd performed. As for going somewhere, that night I went right home. We'd had no money for almost two weeks, and my copy-editing job, a 620-page *Reader's Guide to William Faulkner*, was due the next morning.

In March *Dutchman* began an extended run at the Cherry Lane Theatre, to a flood of outrage at the "raw" language— insignificant today—as well as wide praise. *Newsweek* called it "the most impressive work by an American playwright in the last few years." It won the *Voice* Obie Award for Best Play of 1964. Yet the fact of black anger was most often met with distant, mystified surprise. Even when faced with statistics—a seven-year difference in life expectancy, for instance—whites still refused to acknowledge it. The *Times* was typical: "If this is the way the Negroes really feel . . . there's more rancor buried . . . than anyone can imagine."

Nevertheless there were audiences, more standing ovations, five curtain calls, and some royalties. One day I came upon Roi in the study, reading his reviews. "Appreciating yourself?" I teased.

"It wigs me," he confessed. He was sitting in the rocker,

and I hugged his head to my breast for a moment, rocking and reading. It wigged me too.

And life eased up some. The day-care center took Lisa, who, given equal rights at home, had perceived her exclusion from school as unjust. And although I'd finally become what I'd resisted—a secretary (Roi's)—I liked working for him, especially since we were having an affair. Sometimes I took the kids to school and dashed back home and into bed. It seemed as if we'd weathered so much, and indeed weather, and seasons, and how love comes together were what he wrote about, one of those airy mornings, in his last poem to me.

This was included in his second book of poems, to be published by Grove that coming summer (1964). In his dedication—to Ed Dorn—Roi quoted the theme from the Green Lantern radio program they'd both listened to as children: "In blackest day, in blackest night, no evil shall escape my sight!" Evil was big in our lexicon, and for a short, wonderful while, it was all outside. At 27 Cooper Square things seemed to be fine. I had some time to inspect how I felt, and in a voice that now seems entirely mine, I even managed to catch my household life:

My dearest darling
will you take out
the garbage, the fish heads
the cats
wouldn't eat

the children are sleeping
I cannot hear them breathing

Will you be my friend
and protector from all evil

the dead fish
take them away

please

I never showed Roi this poem, or any of the others I began and saved. Most weren't good enough, but this—my last while we were together—was. By then, though, I was reluctant to love him out loud, unlike all the others who did and had nothing to lose.

21

On a June morning in 1964 we shuffled off for Buffalo, where Roi and Ed Dorn were to teach a summer term at the State University. Four adults and five children squeezed into a two-door sedan: Ed, driving, with Helene and fourteen-year-old Fred holding Lisa, and all the short-legged rest of us—Roi, me, Paul, Chan, and Kellie, overlapped in the back with our feet on the luggage. I fell asleep right after Yonkers.

I'd been up all night, of course, getting us ready. After *Blues People, The Moderns*, and *Dutchman* it seemed as if everyone, from all over, for their own various reasons, wanted to know Roi. The phone was one continuous interruption. The BBC came, and wired the house, and hung a mike inside my dress. Then there were German photographers watching us eat. It wasn't unusual to find, shouting together under the windows, a Japanese jazz buff and a western writer in a ten-gallon hat. Peter Orlovsky, back from India with shoulder-length hair, stayed on our couch awhile; friends came for dinner as always; there was regular Monday-night poker, one game covered by *Life* magazine. In the neglected house I threatened to hire a maid: "*Someone*—cat or person—has shit in this room," I wrote Helene, "and I swear I won't clean it."

Like most men then and now Roi did little to help. But to his credit (and satisfaction) he was supporting us, teaching, reviewing, writing for hours: "*Closeted* for the last four days," I wrote. And at least he took his shirts to the Chinese laundry.

He'd also rented, sight unseen, because we had no car of our own, an expensive house within walking distance of the Buffalo campus, from a professor who was "honored" to have us. Roi didn't tell him we planned to live with the Dorns and split the unaffordable rent. But someone must have been spying. Several days after we moved in, while we were happily gathered at the landlord's large table, he arrived displeased and later tried—unsuccessfully—to evict us.

This was just the beginning of resistance from everyone else, the neighbors as well as the academics. Our interracial "family" was a sign—not always welcome—of the times. The word that summer was *Freedom*. Scrawled on buildings, chanted by marchers: Freedom Now. In Mississippi Freedom Summer, there were Freedom Schools. A flood of young people, black and white, their average age twenty-one, had crowded the South to teach classes and register voters; each was required to bring five hundred dollars for bail; three of them, riding together on a country road, were murdered that June with the help of a deputy sheriff. Fear and suspicion followed northern as well as southern "integrationists."

Crossing to Canada we were stopped and the trunk searched. The questions, the hard eyes, frightened Lisa on my lap. "It's okay," I whispered. But it wasn't.

In July, President Johnson passed the Civil Rights Act Kennedy had initiated, but unenforced it made little difference. Tension continued to build in the South, and in northern communities now called "ghettos." Whenever anyone used the word I flinched. The Buffalo ghetto was wooden, old as the hills; our house wasn't near it. We felt marooned among the white middle-class, Roi of course but the rest of us too. The humid heat clung. It never rained. Helene and I concocted poverty salads, took the kids swimming. That was my thirtieth summer; she was seven years older, married twice and twice as long, still with her loud laugh and long-legged stride. I liked watching her, and Ed too, among whites who disrespected them for being *us*. They never wavered.

Grove Press mailed to Buffalo an advance copy of *The Dead Lecturer*, Roi's new book of poems. He'd kept the dedication to Ed a surprise, and when the package arrived simply handed it to him. "Go ahead, man, open it," Roi said, his face full of mischief. And what a look on Ed, when he read the dedication aloud to the rest of us, shouting the last lines: "Let all who worship evil's might/Beware my power, Green Lantern's light!" Roi was to tell me, soon, that Ed Dorn was the only white man who understood him. It's debatable whether he understood Ed. Like other young blacks he'd asserted himself with a word: he was now black not Negro (knee-grow). Ed had no such magic, only his Green Lantern's light. The year before, he'd addressed this poem to Roi:

Mourning Letter, March 29, 1963

No hesitation
  would stay me

from weeping this morning
for the miners of Hazard Kentucky.
The mine owners'
extortionary skulls
whose eyes are diamonds
don't float
down the rivers, as they should
of the flood

These miners, cold
starved, driven from work, in
their homes float though and float
on the ribbed ships of their frail
bodies,

Oh, go letter,
keep my own misery close to theirs
associate me with no other honor.

The previous fall there'd arrived, from Philadelphia, a magazine called *Black America*. The cartoon on the cover showed a kneeling man labeled "Dr. King and so-called Negro leaders," who was holding papers on nonviolence and saying "Mercy Mercy Mercy" while being bit on the backside by a dog named White Power Structure. Both dog and man were collared, chained, and reined by President Kennedy. Facing them all, raising bumps on Mercy's head with a rolled-up paper ("Freedom Now") and a club ("Nonviolent Reaction"), was the only hero on the set: "Masses and New Afro American Groups."

Max Stanford, the editor, also sent a photograph of himself spread against a car, surrounded by police, with a big knot on his head where they'd clobbered him (for picketing a no-black-workers construction site).

The day all this arrived a group of us were toasting Roi in his study; *Blues People* had just been published and for several days he'd been King of the Hill—interviewed, feted, radio-programmed, fielding compliments about his straight talk, his fighting spirit. He was a little abashed by it all, and suddenly, holding up the photo of Max, he said, "Now *this* . . ."

I gazed at him, fine-tuned to the tone of his voice. I'd heard him shifting gears. Those who risked more than the mimeograph were *right*—and they were new. He couldn't stay King of the Hill by standing still.

"What does he mean?" someone said to me.

"He's worried he'll be replaced," I said, and Roi ducked his head behind that funny little smile of his, the one that always meant I'd peeped him.

In Buffalo, most of a year later, I could still see Max Stanford's bloody head in Roi's head. And more. He'd been in a Town Hall forum with Malcolm X, he'd met with both "Negro leaders" and "black spokesmen." He'd begun to think of himself the way his audiences thought of him, not as a writer but as an "activist." In late July, when Harlem rioted—first of American communities to do so—he flew to New York and would rather have stayed. But he returned to teach his four days a week, a hero to the few black students, and soon, not surprisingly, with a pretty girl on his trail. One evening he mentioned a party some of the students had told him about. When he got ready to go, so did I. But as I was dressing, he said, "You certainly like the role of faculty wife."

In the large, carpeted master bedroom of the real faculty wife, I stood stunned, insulted, half-clothed. He'd never before refused my company. And he counted on my pride. I took off my dress and drank myself to bed. Roi came home upset, of course, reaching for me to put out the fire he knew he'd started. For a moment I clung to him and let myself be soothed. But how could the source of my trouble be my solace? I rolled away, weeping.

From Buffalo he went to a conference in California. I flew to Newark with the children and spent a night at home in

New York. While I was there my father called after six years of silence. He'd intercepted a letter I'd written my mother. "Don't call, don't write," he warned.

Through the painter Larry Rivers we'd rented a cabin on a bay near Southampton for the rest of the summer. Larry also arranged for a rented car. Roi couldn't drive; I'd kept my license for the past ten years to cash checks. Larry met me at the train and then drove me to the car, an old Chevy. I put the children in back and got behind the wheel, peering between the hub and the rim, as I'd done in the only other car I'd ever driven, my father's '52 Chrysler New Yorker. "Now you're all set," Larry said.

For fifteen miles of rough, winding, poorly marked county road my fear was so intense I felt scorched. It had to be useful, I thought. The next day I set myself up with the sofa pillows. Gas was fifteen cents a gallon. The children were game, anytime. We went eighteen miles for ice cream, twenty for a bushel of peaches. We drove to watch the rich on Southampton beach. Everywhere everyone was white, and I was Kellie and Lisa's mother, and that wasn't all. In the parking lot the son of an avant-garde composer-conductor climbed to the top of his father's car and shouted down at Kellie, "I'm the king of the castle, and you're the dirty rascal." She didn't know how to answer. "He called me *dirty*," she sobbed, raising her soft round arms, dark from the sun.

"Um, um, *um*," said Roi, kissing us three when he arrived, then shoving the dresser against the bedroom door to keep out the kids and luring me to bed.

When it was time to leave he suggested I drive home. "But I've never driven in the city," I said. "Oh, you can do it," he said.

I was three when my father carried me screaming into the shower of a public pool in Brooklyn. When the cool, brilliant water hit, my fear just . . . slid . . . into ecstasy— adrenaline? orgasm? I became the girl who would take the plunge. I drove my first bridge—the Queensborough—into

Second Avenue traffic at five in the evening, with my husband seated confidently beside me.

Both these men, Cohen then Jones, first loved me for myself, and then discarded me when that self no longer fit their daughter/wife image. If I hadn't been myself all along I might have been left next to nothing. Still, while they loved me they sometimes saw in me more than I did, and for those times I owe them.

22

In every interview with Roi or review of his work I was mentioned. Sometimes I got a dependent clause: "Jones, who is married to a white woman." Or my name: "his white wife, the former Hettie Cohen." Used against him I blurred his indictments: why in "all you white folks" was I the exception?

By the fall of 1964, black Americans were being asked to make choices. Nearly a decade of nonviolent protest had failed. "They beat me and they beat me with the long, flat blackjack," said Fannie Lou Hamer, on nationwide TV, after all the effort of Freedom Summer hadn't unseated Mississippi's whites-only delegation (to the Democratic National Convention). Black leaders were no longer known only regionally; Malcolm X, minister to New York's Muslims, was photographed in a church in Selma, Alabama, with a sign that said "Your freedom can't wait."

In the seven years I'd been with Roi, I'd watched the loosening of what would one day be called "black rage." I knew it could turn on me but that was part of the risk and I hadn't imagined how much. Now some people were beginning to say that hypocritical Roi talked black but married white. Others, more directly, said he was laying with the Devil.

But this had been—at first—precisely his point, that a black man should be free as any man—to lead his life, to love one and/or attack another, at once. Still, in the new Cedar, only three blocks uptown from the old, the glances of strangers were sideways rather than confrontational. Who was that at the playwright's side—Lula the murderer, his white wife, or the former Hettie Cohen?

And then, as I'd dreaded, one day they all became one.

Dutchman was to be performed at Howard University's homecoming weekend. Bored with typing, as I wrote Helene, "twelve copies of everything in the world" for Roi's latest grant application, I thought it might be fun to go.

Memory's so tricky. All I can see is the open door behind his back. "I can't take you," he said. "I don't want to."

I could feel it coming, like an awful tide. I said "Why?" and then there it was:

"Because you're white."

"As if the tragic world around our 'free zone' had finally swept in and frozen us to the spot," was the way he told it later. My eyes, he said, showed such pain he almost covered his face.

And he should have, I guess, since he'd shattered my life. "But you're not talking about *us*," I said quietly, and then, getting no response, screamed: "You're the only person besides myself I ever trusted—and now *look*! Look where it's *got* me!"

Then I let him go, because I didn't know what else to do. Later I went to a party at the loft of director John Vaccaro. While I was out Roi called every two hours. He'd had a change of heart, thought he'd been wrong. We finally spoke the next day in some desultory way.

He came home humble. I told him he'd forgotten that *we* made the rules. He agreed. "If it's not all right, we'll make it all right," he said. But too late—when he couldn't reach me that night he'd also gone to a party, and met a young black woman who pursued him to New York. Later on she provided, for a while anyway, the image he thought he needed to keep going.

Roi's first full-length play, the one about *Gra, Wal*, and *Eas*, was awaited. He kept saying it had to be retyped. He and I, alone one night, finally read it aloud. This is the play I called Roi's nightmare: the white female character is the black male character's *ex*-wife.

The Slave is about a U.S. race war, set in the future. Walker Vessels, leader of the blacks, has come to the white side under siege by his forces, to confront his ex-wife Grace and her professor-husband, his former literary buddy Easley. Vessels kills Easley, Grace is killed by a bomb, and Vessels himself survives, in rags, broken by war, to tell the tale in flashback. There are children offstage, they probably die too. In between there is much bitterness about what one reviewer called "the interracial crisis we are undergoing."

The play is set in Grace's future—the house where she lives with her new husband. It was she who'd left Vessels, prior to the play, taking their two daughters to the white side after he had taken up arms. It is she who, right at the beginning, calls him "nigger-murderer." It's a tragic breach. He replies: "How long have you been saving that up?"

But their love is the source of the play's tension, all its

emotional grasp. The actress who played the part sent me a marble black-and-white heart, with a card: "Thank you for Grace."

That made me *nuts*.

In production, the nightmare became mine. The man who staged it was the very one who, in 1957, had taken me from *The Threepenny Opera* to his pad on Avenue D, and soured me on a life in the theater. He asked Roi for photos of the children to use in the scenery. An astounded, upset Roi brought home this query, which didn't in the least surprise me. Although Grace is a tall blond WASP, at least one of her lines came from an argument we'd had: "I am not in your head," says Grace, right out of my mouth. "So close to our real lives, so close to that living image," he wrote later.

Later, also, fact and fiction having blurred, he described *The Slave* as a play about "a black would-be revolutionary who splits from his white wife."

While the play was being mounted at the St. Marks Playhouse (with ingenious collapsing scenery by Larry Rivers), I was stuck at home with two cases of chicken pox, unable to catch a rehearsal. I got to the opening night unprepared for the way I'd feel. The last sounds you hear are the children screaming as the house is bombed.

Afterward, in the Ladies', when Gramma caught my eye I burst into tears. But I got myself together and went to the party at Lita Hornick's. "If only you weren't *his* wife," said the man with whom I shared a joint, his arm around me in the elegant bathroom.

I'm in bed, my hungover head under the pillow. Something close by is ringing. The alarm? It's the phone, beside me on the floor. Roi was in bed, now he's not. He must have gone out and left it there. With effort I get it to my ear.

The caller is from the *Saturday Review*. He's old and well known, I studied him at Columbia. He's calling to speak with Mr. Jones.

"Sorry, he's not in." My voice is a blur. What time is it?

"Well, oh dear . . . ," says the drama critic. "Is this his wife?"

"Yes it is."

The critic has a deadline, it seems. "Would *you* . . . answer some questions then?" he says tentatively.

"If I can." I feel feeble and sick, but maybe—*maybe*—I haven't yet lost my mind.

"What does he mean?" says the critic. "I mean, if he's got all this hate, where does that leave us . . . and you?"

The phone presses heavily on the fragile shell of my skull. "Well, first thing, the play's not my life," I say. Even a theater critic knows that.

But he won't let go, he's a dog with a bone. To his distress, I refuse to take Grace's part. "If any white person in the world could, I knew you would understand," Walker says to her. "And then you didn't." I won't dispute his right to say this. The critic and I go round and round. I try to explain the heat of the anger blacks must face and control every day of their lives, how this is really the theme and the tragedy, when people are forced to hate against hate, to the detriment of their mortal souls. Look how Walker Vessels ends up.

Still I don't win my point. My head is wired now, set to explode. At last he says, "Well, thanks a lot, Mrs. Jones, it's been delightful."

I let the receiver fall. Lying there I have almost no substance, as if everything I am, all of *I*—not Lula or Grace but *I, me, now*—has been emptied onto the broad plain of predicament, to be consumed there, cell by cell, in its glare.

The afternoon of Malcolm X's murder, on February 21, 1965, we were drinking champagne at the opening of the new Eighth Street Bookshop, across the street from the old.

Fred McDarrah took a picture of us that appeared on the cover of the *Voice*. Both Roi and I are wearing dark glasses, and in line of nose and lip look alike, intently concealed and not exactly there. He, I know, was also on the paperback aisle, where Vashti, his new girlfriend, was waiting with two of his new friends. These young men, who called themselves poets and functioned as bodyguards, ran errands for Roi and sat with him in endless discussion. I might as well call them lieutenants, for as much as I refused to be Grace, Roi was adapting nicely to Walker Vessels.

Malcolm and he had recently been featured speakers at a rally at Manhattan Center. As soon as Roi heard of the killing he said "Here," handing me his half-full champagne glass, and the next minute, with his entourage, he was gone.

The twenty-four pages of that issue of the *Voice*, with our last family portrait, seem a centrifuge that would send many people and ideas flying the way Roi went out that door: an interview with Malcolm himself only days before his death; Jack Newfield's take on a project in Newark run by Tom Hayden of Students for a Democratic Society (SDS), an organization also active in the recent, first student revolt in Berkeley and in protest against the deepening U.S. involvement in Vietnam. Entertaining that week were Cecil Taylor at Town Hall, John Cage on St. Marks Place, Dick Gregory at the Village Gate, Bill Cosby at the Gaslight. Amid the familiar avant-garde names a couple—Lanford Wilson and Sam Shepard—were new. And besides our photograph on the cover, Roi had all the print he needed, ads for *The Slave* and *The Toilet* and much mention of his new project, the neatly named Black Arts Theater.

This was now his life, his grand new view: Walker Vessels with the right script in his hand. With the promise of a grant he'd bought a building in Harlem, and was enlisting the aid of other black artists in the enterprise. They were offering performances (mostly of Roi's short plays) and classes.

At the time of Malcolm's death, there was also continuing terror and death in the South that would force, finally, a Voting Rights Act. In the course of this struggle there occurred what seemed both a desperate attempt at love, and also the beginning of a clear mistrust between blacks and whites in the civil rights movement. The United States still lived on assumptions: when blacks died the country was shocked; when whites died, it mourned.

All that spring of 1965, Roi came home to read his mail, change his clothes, and make sorrowful love, comparing his situation to that of Jomo Kenyatta, who'd left an English wife to lead the Kenyan people. He'd fumble around his neglected desk; I knew he wasn't writing. He told me he thought he might never write again. What would I think? I told him I didn't think he *could* stop writing.

One night I found him with Lisa, who'd chased him— "I *love* my Daddy"—until she'd got him. She was standing up in her crib in the half-dark bedroom, and he was murmuring softly and caressing her. "Do you think I want to leave my home?" he said when he saw me.

I couldn't tell him that in the long run he'd serve himself better by hanging on, or taking us with him, because I didn't know that. Maybe it never was true. I had nearly begun to doubt it myself. I couldn't bear his *guilt* at being with me, which seemed so shocking when with me he hadn't abandoned but emphasized—and taught—his culture. But I viewed as crucial the collective release of black anger; I wanted that to happen even if my own awkward position continued. I'd seen enough of the South and Harlem and Newark to believe, I thought, in Malcolm's "by any means necessary." "Tell it like it is!" black audiences roared at performances of *Dutchman*. And I couldn't get out of my mind the image of Kellie, sobbing, "He called me *dirty*."

And as in all domestic roiling encumbered or not by public life and racial strife, I didn't know who Roi was telling what. Vashti had rumored they'd be married. I no longer knew what to think.

"So I'm torn," I wrote Helene, "between wanting to continue to live some sort of life, and a genuine desire to remain the faithful loyal stalwart Mrs. Jones."

He's in the doorway, his head on his arm against the frame. The door is open. He's leaving, but he'll be back. "What did you mean," he says, "when you told that reporter it was the wrong time for blacks and whites to be together?"

"I didn't say that, he misquoted me." (As usual.) "We were talking about the new East Village and I said it didn't seem as if interracial bumping and grinding was enough. Like a statement: together for the same old reason—sex."

He and I have just had sex.

"So you think it's the wrong time," he persists.

In the silence, I feel how much he wants me to say this. His sleeve trembles a little as he rubs his head between the long muscle of his shoulder and the doorjamb. Like me he's thin, still a boy really, but neither of us is what we once were. Now it seems we know everything.

I've started to cry. "I didn't mean . . ."

"Don't say anything, don't say anything," he whispers, drawing me to him.

23

There used to be an advertising sign, Gem Blades Cleans Them Clean, painted on the wall of the first tenement on Fifth Street. From my kitchen window you could sit and stare at it, lost in your thoughts or holding them off, your eye recording over and over, Gem Blades Cleans Them Clean. The thing was so present, and faded so slowly, that I never imagined it altogether gone. Like Roi. But one day he arrived and handed me a piece of paper on which he'd typed, because he couldn't say it: "I think we should talk about a divorce."

Better dead than Grace, I thought. It was his idea and would have to be his fault. "I will never divorce you," I said heroically.

So there was a scandal downtown: LeRoi Jones Has Left His White Wife. It fit right in with dissolving black-white political alliances, as he later wrote: "What was the correlative or parallel scene being played all over the world which meant the same thing in all the different sectors and levels of human experience?" Close to home, though, it hurt most. There was pressure on all black people to end their interracial relationships. A.B. Spellman, whose wife was pregnant, had a terrible time and finally left after his son was born. Years later Roi met a woman who accused him of single-handedly forcing her husband from her. "It *was* sad," he admitted.

Having grown to like him the neighborhood missed him. Our mail carrier was a Brit who'd married a Puerto Rican during the Second World War and lived on the Lower East Side. He loved the worldliness of what he brought to our door, anything U.K. or European. When I told him how to split it all up he looked hurt.

When you're sorry enough for yourself, the weight of other people's pity seems unbearable. On top of it rode anger and disappointment. I felt battered, as if all the talk and emotion were attempts to *reshape* me.

One night I was at the Five Spot watching gray-haired Teddy Wilson play the piano, thinking of Roi's parents, and the children, and how they would have to live with all this, when a group of painters arrived. In a recently published poem, Roi had called on "Black dada nihilismus" to murder his friends, all of whom were now upset and angry, unprepared for the position in which he'd put them. Like Ed Dorn, they had no name for the way they were white. Neither did I.

Nevertheless I felt stranded among them, and bitter at being expected to have a position on Roi, just like any other white person. Divorced, I could no longer plead immunity. I could be persuaded to testify.

"How could he," they said.

"He felt he had to," I said. That sounded right, I

thought, and let alone the question of whether he'd wanted to.

"It would have been easier to die," I wrote Helene, "except for the kids." When school was out I took them to the beach. They were agile and strong and could scale the high partition that divided their room from mine. Mornings my opening eye would discover them grinning down at me from the ceiling. They didn't speak of missing their father, though I knew they did. "You can't go," Kellie had said to him, "you're one of the funny things." Still they'd lived among so many sympathetic adults that all they needed, I thought, was a steady supply. But of whom?

The coin has jammed in the phone because of the sand, which is everywhere in little dunes, in the corners of the roadside phone booth, up to the edge of the field of Bridgehampton scrub. If I stay here long enough it will cover me too and then this call won't be so hard to make because I'll be dead. But the children are bouncing impatiently in the backseat of the car. I bang the quarter in and dial the Newark number.

"Where have you *been!*" Gramma says. She's angry and anxious. Why haven't I *called!* Where have I taken her babies? She's been looking for me for weeks. *Weeks.* "I've been out of my mind," she says.

I tell her I have been too, and why: Roi is in Mexico, divorcing me.

"Well, *I'm* not divorcing you."

Not a beat has been skipped. I can't speak.

"Are you okay?" she says gently.

"Everyone around here—except me—thinks Roi will come home one day," I wrote Helene. "I think nothing will bring him back except a miracle or a terrible disaster to his plans uptown." Expecting neither, and hoping to break the power of his absence, I moved myself into his room and put my bed in place of the *Record Changer*'s rolltop desk. But the past crept into the new dust, and at night I lay remembering the desk in every location—Nat Hentoff slouched on it in the narrow stuffy store on Sullivan Street, Joel Oppenheimer asleep on it on Twentieth Street. My history, vanished.

Whenever Roi came to take the children he would speak to me from across the room, as if he didn't want to get a good look. Then one morning, in what had been our bedroom, he cornered me in his wordless way of asking and bent shyly to kiss me. Surprised, I lifted a hand to touch his face. But he withdrew in pain—he'd had a tooth pulled.

A tooth! A part of him—as I'd known him—was *gone*. I told him how strange this felt.

"But I'm the same person," he said quietly, as if he were hoping. "The same person, just in another place," he said. In my rearranged rooms I felt the same way. There was a sad relief in our embrace.

Now here is again, my ex-husband, back like a song. It's getting colder, the money's slower, I'm working as a proofreader. Roi comes around to go to bed, as if he needs to get warm. He won't talk about anything. We lie there in the noontime light while tailpipes clang into the basement. What is he thinking? He looks so tired and bugged.

"Maybe someday you and Vashti and I will all live together," he says.

There was a time I regretted my quick refusal. I didn't stop for a long vision, to consider the possibilities—that I was the one with staying power, that he might want to come home, as everyone had predicted. Instead I merely said what I thought at the moment, my usual instinctive grasp at the future, and that situation wasn't in it.

"No, Roi, I don't think so," I said.

△ △ △

I spotted them as I came up the street, four guys in suits in a car in front of the house. As soon as I had the children inside they all got out at once, Hollywood style. Two of them flanked me while the third slid in ahead and the fourth flipped a badge. "Mrs. Jones," he said.

It's frightening to be surrounded in such a swift, practiced manner. The kids were scared too, and I wanted them out of earshot of whatever this was. "Here's the key, go upstairs, it's okay," I said to them. They didn't move.

"We won't hurt your mother," said the man who had spoken.

But they stood their ground, Kellie Jones age six and Lisa Jones age four. Their fear controlled, their sober, judging faces calm, they were, in miniature here, the way they would always have to be. And they've never let me down. We had a code: "It's *really* okay," I said, and they went.

"You're the wife of LeRoi Jones?"

"*Ex*-wife," I corrected.

"Is he here?"

"No. Why?"

"He's been reported missing."

"Who reported that?"

This, I was told, was classified.

"Well, he's missing from here, too," I said. "So I guess it's your job to find him."

They don't want to accept this, but they don't have a search warrant either. They fill the hall with their suspicion and contempt. When they leave I see that one has a big streak of whitewash from our wall on his sleeve, I hope he never gets it off.

Now I'm in Newark, the mushy spring of 1966. Roi and I are on his parents' porch. The Black Arts is over, the building raided, the guns of the poet-bodyguards discovered and seized. Roi has run away to his parents. No longer with Vashti, he's sort of with a very young woman. He hasn't any money to give me, hasn't had any for months. His clothes hang on bones, his dapper pride seems gone. I'm ashamed for him as much as angry.

I ask him, "What did you really want, those times, did you want to come home?"

"I was . . . confused," he says.

He looks much more confused now. He looks nervous and haunted and angry. But he doesn't look sorry, and that's what I notice. And that's what I'll remember, because this was the last time we spoke, as *us*, and we left it right there.

A few weeks later I ran into Allen Ginsberg on Avenue B. I hadn't seen him in a year, and he felt terribly guilty at having been in India when Roi left.

"Why didn't you *stop* him!" Allen demanded.

To protect our female family, our friend the saxophonist Marion Brown gave us a male dog. Training him I acquired a number of summonses. On the morning of Kellie's seventh birthday, as I turned to lock the street door, two policemen rounded the corner. "Wait," one of them said, his hand in my face. "Have you paid your summonses, Mrs. Jones?"

I'd never seen these men in my life. Neither had given me a summons.

"Have you paid?" the cop repeated.

"Yes," I lied.

The cakebox I was holding bent against my chest as he backed me up to the door. "You're lying," he said, and then, "You wait right here, because you're under arrest."

Then the two of them burst out laughing and went on toward the precinct, and I delivered the cake to the class party, and then called Marion, who promised to pay the summonses immediately, and tried to calm me. But I shut myself into the dirty phone booth and cried—the hottest, bitterest tears I'd ever tasted.

It wasn't until the following year that I was actually arrested—for a ten-dollar outstanding ticket—but by then I had a boss who could bail me out and I was used to the notice I got as Roi's ex-wife. This was just about the time his head was finally busted. He's passed the test, I thought when I saw the pictures of him dripping blood. In Newark, where he was living and working, he'd started out visible and worked upward. He was with the woman who'd become his second wife. As if to refute the fact that he'd ever settled elsewhere, his new book, a collection of essays, was titled *Home*. He would neither speak to me nor send money, and wrote instructing me to reach him only through his parents. He did not call the children; they were driven to see him by emissaries. Eventually he changed his name to Imamu Amiri Baraka, and someone told me, though I never saw it, of a newspaper interview in which he denied my existence.

But if I'd been abandoned I hadn't been removed, and everyone else in this house remained. The new East Village became an active and crowded bohemia, at a time when young people all over the country were beginning to move. North as well as South, there were crowds that required control. Our house was still watched. When Archie's groups rehearsed, people who gathered were dispersed. One night his studio was raided twice, the second time by police in full riot gear, who then gave him a five-dollar summons for disturbing the peace.

On quieter nights, leaving the children to Garth Shepp's ear, I went out and lost myself here and there. But people projected their dreams of Roi beside me. Visions of him watched me from his white friends' sad eyes. At the last party I ever attended at Lita Hornick's, in all those crowded rooms there was only one black person, the man I'd brought. "Why don't you just stop *thinking*," said Basil King. That would be the deathblow, I thought. "I think I'm going to be all right," I wrote Helene with plenty of doubt.

And I tried—with margin for relapse—to stick to what I expected of this new, third, self, Mrs. Hettie Jones, my proper form of address according to the *Chicago Manual of Style*. I liked it—not least because it was easier having the same name as the children in schools, hospitals, settlement houses, and all the other institutions we had to rely on.

It would be fifty dollars, said the operator, to change the name in the phone book.

"Fifty *dollars*?" I said.

"Well, if you want a phone in your name, you have to open an account and pay a deposit."

"But listen, I've always paid the bills, you can verify that, can't you? You have my signature, there was a joint account and I signed the checks. . . ."

"Well, I'm sorry."

"But are you sure? I mean . . . I'm paying the bills on this phone—this is *my damn phone*—are you going to take it away now? Because I asked? Because I said I got divorced? Are you going to—"

"Mrs. Jones?"

". . . Yes."

"I have an idea. We'll keep the old listing, but we'll send the bills to him care of you. So your bills will say E. L. Jones, care of . . . Care of whom? How do you want it?"

Anger has seized my throat. At last I choke out: "C-care of . . . *Mrs.* Hettie Jones."

Then, suddenly hearing it, a veil lifts, I realize I've married . . . *myself*!

One summer morning not long after, in Katz's Delicatessen on Houston Street, I had a conversation about race with a social worker. I was interviewing him, for a book I was helping to write, a history of the antipoverty agency Mobilization for Youth. I'd been collecting stories, many from women alone with children. Poverty, it seemed, looked just like me.

But it's race that concerns the social worker. It matters, he says, every minute all the time, don't be naïve.

Katz's is unchanged, like the rest of this street I'd first seen from my father's car. I'm thinking of my mother, who recently met me here, and sat between the children, a hand on each little thigh. "Oh, so soft," she'd crooned. What color was that? She'd forgotten.

"If you wake up and race is a given," I say to the social worker, "it's gone while you're looking for your socks."

His face reddens. He thinks I'm trivializing the issue, but knowing my story he indulges me—out of decency. "I'm saying this time will pass," I insist, staring past him. It must, I think. To believe otherwise is perverse and irrational and would kill me.

Outside it's not the hip East Village but the faded brick of Loisaida, the Spanish-English version of Lower East Side. This is my home, and if my life resembles that of this man's clients more than it does his own, like them I also have my pride. I wait patiently for my anguish to subside, by now I know it will.

Hairs keep surfacing in this house, blond to black, kink to straight, no two alike. I'm the super here now—the other day I tarred one into the roof. The view from up there is changed: a fourteen-story building looms in the sky above where the Five Spot used to be, and these streets have been home to hippies, yippies, punks, yuppies, buppies, and—at last!—Sonny Rollins's Mohawk haircut. E. Vill., on the map now, is a legend of several generations. "You're a *relic!*" cried an old friend, accurately.

Without a *him* in the house, there was of course more

space/time for *her*, and I tried to redefine the way a woman might use it. I'd maintained ties to the neighborhood settlement where the children had been in day care, and after the Mobilization book was done I helped design, and then directed, a large after-school program there and in all the other Lower East Side settlement houses. In my twenty-five-dollar '53 Plymouth, I cruised the neighborhood minding several hundred second-graders, teenage tutors, social workers, and teachers. This meant a curriculum; I also wrote evaluations for Head Start programs and after-school programs modeled on the one we'd started at MFY. I wrote all the time and never thought of myself as a writer.

Malcolm X had advised white people to work for the black struggle in their own communities. Another census was coming up then: the seventies were upon us. What race household would we be this time? In what community? Without Roi, mine seemed less than ever the male-dominated art world. And it seemed a more healing life to leave the past to itself, seal it off so it couldn't hurt, as I wrote in a poem to Helene, after her divorce, "Become a pearl / of a girl / Yeah, momma." (I never foresaw how this move would erase me. In the 1983 *Dictionary of Literary Biography* volume on the Beats, Hettie Jones, the author by then of a dozen books for children, would appear once again as his white wife, Hettie Cohen.)

As always, occasionally late at night there were poems to throw into the box. I was sure—I *am* sure—that nothing but my own voice held me hostage. I was learning, I think, as fast as I could:

> *It's okay, isn't it, if you get there*
> *after the clothes dryer that squeaks*
> *when it stops like Inner Sanctum*
> *When I was five they*
> *listened downstairs but I was too frightened*
> *get out of bed*

234

get up, it's only
a radio
The poems are frightening I can
never get up . . .

I tried other men but none lasted. No one was smart or funny or ambitious enough, and though desired I was also untouchable, a woman living, as I later wrote, "in the middle of other people's wars." One summer the children went to visit school friends in Vermont for a couple of weeks. I drove to fetch them with the father of the family, a Jewish professional who thought my life interesting. "So when did you first begin to like black men?" he asked.

We had stopped along the road to see some fossilized dinosaur tracks. I was standing in one and felt as extinct as the being who'd left it, thinking of the men of every race I'd loved.

"But don't you *see* . . . ," I began.

The light fades.
Where will I put all my joy?
What's to be done when I'm tired of celebration,
tired of autumn, tired of Christmas, oh
if there were one man, as there once was
whose eyes cut through the seasons

The single-parent-head-of-household rises early. At eight-thirty on a spring morning in 1969, I'd already dropped the children at school and was in my car having a quiet cup of coffee outside the white-columned Mobilization for Youth building, a former wedding palace on East Second Street. I'd learned, the previous afternoon, that my job would end, that antipoverty was turning pro-, and I was sunk in the plushy green Plymouth, willing fierce thoughts about *next*, when a young couple passed, wrapped in each other's arms, as if they'd risen from bed like that and walked out the door.

It was a warm day and through my open window they even smelled of love.

At once I was dead sure I'd never marry again. But then on a sudden, wonderful, liberating wave—completely unexpected—the heavy knot of regret rose from my breast and flew out the window. Great joy in the morning! I was thirty-five years old and no longer needed what women were taught to live for! I jumped from the car and went running upstairs, singing: "Hello young lovers. . . ."

The quiet, kind man who was my boss had chosen that morning to arrive early. He appeared at my door.

"Don't you *see*?" I exulted.

M y first book for children was an easy reader about the Montgomery, Alabama, bus boycott. ("No," said Mrs. Rosa Parks, "I will not get up.") Too close to those times, it was bought but never published. Soon, though, I had some stories in textbooks, and my second book, *The Trees Stand Shining*, a collection of Native American poems, came out in 1971. I went on from there, living hand-to-mouth on small advances, and my fifth and favorite effort, *Big Star Fallin' Mama*, was named one of 1974's best young adult books by the New York Public Library. It was dedicated to Anna Lois Russ Jones, once the second-fastest woman in the world and absolutely its fastest Gramma, who, true to her word and along with her husband Coyt Leroy Jones, had never divorced either myself or the grandchildren they loved.

Like the first four, this book was written by Hettie Jones, a relatively new person in America, who under the lunacy of apartheid would have become colored—classified "down" when she married and had children, although the actual experience can best be described as broadening. "The angle is bent, the light refracted, the sightlines reconstructed," I wrote in one of the stories I began to publish in the seventies.

But if mothering Kellie and Lisa has been the lifetime lesson I'd predicted, it's also been more delight than I could've imagined. They've been themselves forever, and, even more than I, each has made herself up, has seized and expanded the possibilities for life as a "person of color." In 1981, speaking at her college graduation, Kellie said: "Here I've been your 'minority student,' but don't forget I'm the world's majority." And Lisa, appearing with Kellie on a recent panel at New York's New Museum of Contemporary Art: "The myth of the American mulatto as perpetual outsider, cast helplessly between two bloodlines, forever conflicted with no allegiances, only denies the authority of black culture and the empowering sense of black identity in an American and world community."

Before Roi left he'd written me a note about the "decadent and despairing" East Village. What would become of his children? he asked. Perhaps he couldn't envision a neighborhood grown around us. But the black artists who stayed downtown after he left eventually put the old places to new uses: the painter Joe Overstreet, with his wife Corinne Jennings, runs Kenkeleba House gallery in the Mobilization building where I worked; their bedroom was my office. I still run into Ornette Coleman on the street, and all the others whose names I haven't had space to mention here. We were all waiting when the seventies brought another, multiracial, bohemia. "*Well!*" said one splendidly confident Asian to me then, "We know it ain't about *race* anymore."

But it is, of course, into the nineties, in new and different ways.

As Amiri Baraka, Roi has sometimes recrossed the river, where the "black dada nihilismus" of his poem hasn't—yet?— murdered his old friends. But if this rage had *not* been expressed? I've come to see those times—and the psychological advances of the Black Power movement—as a necessary phase in African-American, and ultimately American, history. If the contrary could be argued, I haven't troubled myself to invent it.

I also don't regret my independence, but whether Roi was wrong to leave me then is less important than that such a move, for those reasons, would be useless now. Too many of us unnamed—light and dark—inhabit these woods. African-American is one specific history; there's more, and no easy answer. "I am as any other sad man here / american," he wrote. As always it's not the past but *next* I'm chasing.

It was a while before I dragged the old poems out of their box and wrote new ones, and read them in public along with my stories, and began to think of myself as the writer whose name is on this book. There was a pivotal moment, though, a cloudy day in the winter of 1973. I had rounded the corner of the St. Marks churchyard, bundled up, booted, my hat pulled low, just another small dark woman in the Western Hemisphere. Disguised, I thought, against the endless regrets, the questions. Do you ever see Roi? How about the children?

The churchyard is fenced, and a nursery group was playing there. One of the teachers turned and looked out at me as I passed along Second Avenue.

I remembered him. He'd clerked in the old Eighth Street Bookshop.

He wanted to recognize me, too, though it was hard to get past my intent withdrawal. He came to the fence politely. "Are you . . . ," he asked, and I waited, caught.

"Are you still . . . ," he tried again. By this time I knew what he was thinking, it wasn't an unfamiliar scene. He was searching out a name for me and rejecting all the choices. Is she Cohen? No, she was Jones. Is she yet that, or is the name removed like the man from whom she got it?

I smiled. I'd help if I could.

But then he came out with it, what he'd decided to ask—
and it was a smash!

"Are you still . . . Hettie?" he said.

"By all means," I said laughing. By all means.